WALL

Ellen Phethean

STACK
BOOKS

Published 2007
by

Smokestack Books
PO Box 408, Middlesbrough TS5 6WA
e-mail : info@smokestack-books.co.uk
www.smokestack-books.co.uk

Cover design by James Cianciaruso

Printed by
EPW Print & Design Ltd

ISBN 0-9551061-6-8
ISBN 978-0-95510616-3

Smokestack Books
gratefully acknowledges the support of
Middlesbrough Borough Council
and Arts Council North East

Smokestack Books is a member of
Independent Northern Publishers
www.northernpublishers.co.uk
and is represented by Inpress Ltd
www.inpressbooks.co.uk

Published 2007
by

**STACK
BOOKS**

Smokestack Books
PO Box 408, Middlesbrough TS5 6WA
e-mail : info@smokestack-books.co.uk
www.smokestack-books.co.uk

Cover design by James Cianciaruso

Printed by
EPW Print & Design Ltd

ISBN 0-9551061-6-8
ISBN 978-0-95510616-3

Smokestack Books
gratefully acknowledges the support of
Middlesbrough Borough Council
and Arts Council North East

Smokestack Books is a member of
Independent Northern Publishers
www.northernpublishers.co.uk
and is represented by Inpress Ltd
www.inpressbooks.co.uk

Kylie

I often stare out
me bedroom window. I can see
a gang of lads and lasses: they look small
from up here. They hang about, nothing to do
nowhere to go, cannot kick a ball even
so they sit, wait, smoke, swear, laugh and drink
scaring the bairns, the old folks as they call out.
Mam says they're animals, they're not, nah.
She says it's a jungle, the bushes grow too tall
you might get jumped on by chava's
rapists, smackheads, or what all.
People say it's rough. Nah, its not that bad
I should kna, I live here, in the Byker Wall.

Kylie looks out of her window at night

Sometimes
I lie in bed with the curtains open
before the moon rises.
On a clear night yer might see one
travellin ever so slowly
remote and cold
like those mini diamond ear studs in the sky
not stars;
Dad pointed one out to me
once up the coast
we were on a long sandy dune
with only the sound of the surf
and a huge black sky:
You have to be patient, he said
to look, and wait. And
if yer lucky, yer see
a little pin point of light
moving through the stars
in a steady line. And we did.
That's a satellite, he said.
Just imagine it whizzing messages around the world
could be from Australia
or Aberdeen.
A radio wave bounces off the earth, up
into space, hits the satellite dish
it's like a bat, bounces the wave back
to another part of the earth.
Just remember that, he said
When your troubles seem too big.

Which surprised me
cos normally all Dad sees in the sky
is pigeons.

Me troubles

Me Granda died six month ago,
it feels like yesterday,
like forever.

Everything fell apart:
Mam got down, Sean got wilder;
Granda was the only one could stop him.
Dad. Well. He's just Dad.
And I felt lost.
Like when things yer rely on,
yer cannot trust them no more.

But Nana, she's been solid
as a wall, stronger than all of us.
I divvent kna what I'd de if she wasn't there.

Take Mam.
When it comes to her
I might as well be a switched off moby
or madc of glass
or a tv with the sound down;

I might as well be dead.
Sean's all she's bothered about.

Sean's me big brother,
he never sits still, he's never quiet
he's like a tidal wave takin over
yer cannot avoid him
he's everywhere taking up space
getting into trouble.
Never bin to school since he was 12
since Mr Cairns
made him sit in the Removal Unit
all day til 4 o'clock. No Break,
no dinnertime. Just sitting.

Did his head in, so much sitting still.
All because he threw a book
and swore. In the end he broke a chair.
Mam says he didn't mean to.
He couldn't help it. He's hyper.
There's all sorts of words for Sean
but basically when he's on a radge, he's mental.
I tell you, it drives me mental
when he comes in my room
fiddles with me stuff.
Cack-handed, breaks things
just by pickin them up.
An he's crap at reading an writin,
He's got other skills,
Mam says. Yeah
like twistin her round his little finger
he's mint at that.
He'd win prizes the way he acts sweet
and she'd be first to hand em out.

But me ?
If I get wrong off the teachers
Mam hoys a fit
or if I get a good report
she says. Oh Aye ?
like I just said
it's raining.
She's more interested
in Coronation Street
than she is in me,
I'm tellin yer. It's shit.
So. I say nowt.
No point.

Kylie goes down Raby Street Youth Centre

She's thin and hard as a table leg
with lacquered hair, curls like a sloth in a chair,
until she's asked if she wants to participate
in a discussion on a Teen Shelter
then she's a pebble shot from a catapult
dangerous and accurate:
Nah
I'm not doin it.
Ask her - she'll talk.
S'daft man.
I'm not makin a fool of meself.
Got nowt to say.
Ask them. Them lads are mouthy
got too much to say
I hate it here, me
s'boring
I'd rather be down the Dene any day
hanging out.
Nah
I'm not saying nowt.
I'm going forra tab.

She likes Scotty, but keeps it to herself.
Silence protects her like a wall :
no secrets get out, no pain gets in.
Say nowt, and nowt'll happen.

Sean's tag

Attention Deficit Hyperactivity Disorder, Dyslexia,
Special Needs Removal Unit, Caution, Custody, Persistent
Youth Offender, Acceptable Behaviour Agreement, Criminal
Damage, Racially Aggravated Burglary, Anti Social
Behaviour Order, Crime and Disorder Act, Anger
Management Course, Intensive Supervision

Sean's head swims with words
they've always been his enemy
won't stay still on the page
like black demons or matchstick men
that hop in front of his eyes, like fleas
teasing him, moving their little letters about
making a fool of him, making others laugh at him
infuriating him.
Until he discovered a way to make them do what he wanted.

If the page was big enough, the letters bold enough
the colours not black, but crimson, emerald, silver and jet
with spray paint and a blank wall
Sean could write his tag, his name
with care, detail, artistic flair,
A'CEE
and other words too, words the whole of Newcastle
could read.

School, the Polis, Adults, Everyone
said he was no good, a failure, the worst
So Sean said Right, I'll be the Best
at being Bad.
It is his message to the world.

Sean aka A'CEE

Sean's haircut is a number one
he's banana nosed, it curves from a childhood fall
jumping out of bed
he's got a big smile, a mobile expression
his mouth's a squashed strawberry
fleshy and red

with a can of spray paint in his hand
and a picture in his head, he's happy

but often he's on a come down,
after a night of clubbing, dope and alcohol
he can't get out of bed
full of aimless anger, he's all aggression
his mood is dangerous, raw,
his eyes very red

then he hates the world
and
he hates himself

Sean's piece of graffiti

I did this sweet piece
side of Dallas Carpets Warehouse
ten foot by four
Massive - it was Bad !
A'CEE in black wildstyle
with a blood red infill
and a green fade.

It was up for days
yer couldn't miss it, man
could see it for miles
from Byker Bridge Metro
the top of Tom Collins
all ower.
My Tag – A'CEE
King of Byker,
Bad, that's me.

Mam

has oven-roasted hair
oyster shell eyes, grey and ridged
her body is a comfy sofa, welcoming
but saggy from use, she waves a tab:
The Polis caught him red-handed
aye, and a mean red
a can a spray paint in his hand
an his sign, his tag
wet on the wall A'CEE.
The others had scattered,
buzzin, he was. Off it,
full of summat,
laughin his head off,
never saw the bizzies til too late
and language ? oh the air was blue
effin this and calling them
the black bastards. I coulda died
of embarrassment. They called for me,
him shouting his heed off in the van,
in front of all the neighbours:
Will yer come to the station, Missus ?
they asked. They know Sean
gets a bit excited when he's mixed it
EE's and spliffs and Fosters.
He couldn't hold the pen still
to sign his name, bit the stick
in two for the DNA test
spat it out, told them to stick it
the other end.
But he means no harm.
I mean, graffiti ?
It's not like muggin old wifies
is it ? Even has artistic possibilities
so I've heard.
I can't see it meself, like,

and I'm sure they're all sick of it
round here. No wall or door way
is safe.
The thing is, it's like leaving your fingerprints
all ower the scene of the crime:-
the Polis know whose tag's whose.
But that's the point, Sean says
somewhere public, big,
then everyone knows it was you,
graffiti artists are famous, he says
in America.
Aye, I say and this isn't
the Big Cox's Orange Pippin is it ?
Wake up I say, but
he takes no notice of the likes of me
takes after his Dad,
he's a fool an all. Feckless.
Mind I love him to bits
Sean's always been a lovely lad
wild and reckless
but lovely. Big cheeky smile
could make me laugh, even when I wer cross.

But this is his second time in court
yer cannot get away with it like yer did
I tell him, the council sent a letter
we'll get chucked oot if you don't behave.
This is serious, Sean, I tell him.

His Granda had the knack, could make Sean listen,
calm down, just with his tone of voice.

Mebbes I've been too soft on him ?
But life's hard for the young ones.
Education did nowt for im,
and there's nee work; they can all see that.
What's the point of learnin

when there's nowt to learn for ?
That's what our Sean says.
I just sigh; stare out the window, thinkin
what this street used to be like
when I was his age.

Scotty

likes Decks, djs and dancing all night
is hanger-thin, clothes but no substance
eyes like bruised plums
and a mouth as wide as the Tyne Tunnel.
He talks as he walks, head full of beats:

Walkin down the street
walkin to the beat
feeling Mint, feeling cool
M nobodiz fool.
Gotta rocket in m pocket
n'm gonna see the lads
gotta door ? better lockit
coz the lads are trubble bad
we z tuff, we c'n hackit,
n the bizzies mek z mad
we z winnaz, betta back it,
or we'll mek you wish you had.

Scotty gets a gig

Haway, Sean, I've been booked
MCing at the Blue Diz-zee.

The club by the coast
does the Underground sound.

Aye.   Next week, it'll be sweet
Nee alcohol, just water. All ncct.

Nee bother, we can meet
Lee in the park first, have a bong.

Aye. Will yer tell Kylie
get her mates to come along ?

Kylie and Sean

Mam, tell him !
he's in me room
tell him, Mam
he's messin with me Toon Top !
Piss off Sean
you get on my tits.
Piss off Sean
leave my friggin little bits.
Piss off will yer ?
Get out of my space.
Piss off Sean
I'm sick of your face.

Alreet, I'll not tell you then
about Scotty
doing Decks at the Blue Diz-zee next week,
all nighter.
Bet you're gannin down the Youth Club the neet ?
Scaby Raby Street ?

Piss off Sean

Piss off yerself, I'm gannin down the dene
ter meet Lee.

Dad down the Ouseburn pigeon crees

has a forgotten air, left there
by history going in another direction;
his glasses held with elastoplast,
his good jacket dusty
now just a remnant of that other life.
Dad has a view of river
through a gap in rooves.
He talks to pigeons, not us, complains Sean.
High up Dad flies on a dandelion and chickweed carpet
bound by concrete and iron railings.
Crees built by the council for £3,000
shocking Mam who can't get a window fixed.
The taste of a threepenny bit
it's weight, how many sides,
these I remember...
my wife's voice,
the birth of Sean
the foreman's parting words;
I cannot bring these to mind,
Dad whispers to a cooing breast.

Sean can't remember the word
logarithms, ships at the end
of the street, sherbet dips,
he's forgotten when
his Dad stopped bringing
surprises home from work.
Sean lives on street cred below,
he's lost something
but doesn't know.
He's never needed to use his eyes,
Dad says, releasing the pigeon,
not like us.
Sean says, I know how to ride in cars
and to look out for my mates,
one day I'll take off so fast.

Dad wipes his hands and says nothing,
rubs his glasses on his shirt and sits
on an old chair from the tip.

Kylie's his little pigeon
first time he held her in that pink hospital room
and cooed to her, she beamed for him
Mam was scornful, said it was wind
Newborn bairns cannot smile
but he was sure.

She's bonny, and she's canny with school work.
But is she canny enough ? There's plenty of scallys
that'll try and pull her off course.
And he watches the Ouseburn
fill with tidal water, making the small red
and blue boats bob, then float.
He whistles Bobby Shaftoe
through his teeth.

Dad's story

I was born at the end of the war
like thoosans of others - men coming back:
Boom - lots of little bairns.

Of course, we all grew up,
lads together, playing games
on bomb sites, bogey's down the bank

then we all left school together
so yer had to be top of the class
to get the job yer wanted:

TV engineer. Telly was the big new thing.
Yer got a van wi that job.
But I was third from top.

So I got an apprenticeship
in the shipyards - Fitter and Turner
when I turned twenty one.

Mind, it was hard work
seven thirty in the morn,
fog drifting off the Tyne,

that metal ship's belly
was icy cold, so the lads
would set a welding rod

strike an arc against the bulk head
and leave it, glowing,
like a one bar electric fire.

Against the rules, like
but hey, when did the rules
ever work for us, eh ?

It was like that wi her too;
I wasn' her top choice,
but Jack went off to Australia.

So, she married me.
But I was always second best
I think she regretted it.

Then things changed at work
big ships being built abroad, cheaper.
Yards closing, like the mines, the steelworks

a right epidemic it was: I lost my job
too, then she kicked me oot
said she didn't want me

under her feet. But she
changed her mind when
she saw how much Benefit

two households can get.
Now we're neither one
thing nor the other.

She lets me sleep and eat
at home, but I spend all day
at the crees. I've got the keys

to the other flat, but
I'm never really there.
I'm not really anywhere.

It breaks me up to see Sean
going the same way
only faster, younger.

The Asylum Seeker's family

Mr Jayasinha and his wife are hot house flowers
transplanted into a northern rockery,
they struggle in the cold climate.

Their boy stares with marble eyes
his mouth a thin wall of defiance:
Papa speaks loud to our neighbours,
but they don't understand.
I talk in whispers but they don't hear.
They think we are stupid, call us Paki.
But we are from a country they have never heard of.

Surrounded by those who do not know
the geography of east or west
except in their own city, who go no further
than Macdonald's and think beyond the wall is enemy territory,
this family has travelled over oceans and mountains
to seek refuge.

Their boy struggles to learn English,
he already speaks
two other languages; at School
some in his class cannot read or write.
They are angry and say they will beat me.
Mr Jayasinha soothes his son, but frets and muses
We left because of such threats.

Mrs Jayasinha likes her new home, speaks to the kind lady
a few doors down:
Why do some people here spoil their country ?
the trees, the grass, so green
why do they burn cars there, hn ?

Well, hen, there's good and bad everywhere.
Generally Geordies are friendly folk,
I found that, when I first came, like you
young, and a stranger to this town.

Nana

came from Scotland and married a man from Walker
She's never told the secret she carried with her.
Her body's taut, a roly-poly sausage
skinned by tight cream leggings, a man's cardigan
round her undulating figure, stomach like a bun.
Surprising like a golden dram of whiskey
that slips down easily, then burns,
she talks of lochs and brogues, a foreign tongue
lilting in her throat, softly sung:
Awa wi yer, ma wee bairns.
There's no such thing as no work.
We all do it, d'you ken,
although our tools may be unnoticed.
Nappy pin or rivet, pliers, spoon or pen
all worked by human hands,
tools don't discriminate,
only minds do, hen.
Sometimes there's no call for our work
or no pay, but still we do it
for love and dignity,
we do it for ourselves.

But she knows that it's hard to understand
when poverty and lack don't mean
what they did back then:
No breakfast and no shoes - but we didne know
any different, no-one told us we were poor.
Oor riches were a house full o' laughter
and freedom te roam.
These young folk don't listen,
they've all got those ear plugs,
heads full o' noise, never been anywhere,
can't see past the end of their noses.
No pride or skill like my man had.

Life in the wall

Dad sees
A Vee sign above
geese giving two fingers
to Autumn.

Mam listens to
raised voices in the back lane,
black and yellow bags bulge - lives
thin with stretching too little too far.

Sean loves the whine,
off-road bikes, bad lads
shooting through the estate.

Nana imagines she hears
the rush of waves
in the cars, endlessly passing.

In a high wind
the flat shakes
Kylie
dreams of escape.

The Jayasinha son learns
not to go out
when he hears
lads shout:
TOON TOON
BLACK AND WHITE ARMEE !

Kylie goes to school

So. Kylie has honoured us with her presence this morning
what time do you call this, spit that gum out please and
Will You Take Those Things out of Your Ears. Now.
I'll take that walkman. How
do you expect to hear what I'm teaching
thank you
where's your assignment ?
coursework ?
Homework ?
Tuck that shirt in, are those regulation earrings ? I don't think so
Sit up, don't slouch Wake Up Are You Listening to Me
What sort of Attitude is that Young Lady ?
Don't answer back I will not tolerate language in my English Lesson
is that how you talk to your mother at home ?
quiet the rest of you that's quite enough Kylie
I'm not having that sort of thing in my class
thank you very much
Off to see the Head of Year Now

Now Kylie,
do you know why your English Teacher has sent you to see me ?
Let's have a look at your record, not very impressive
Is it ?
Oh Kylie, Kylie, you were doing so well last year
What's Happened ?
you know you're quite capable of some decent grades if you
Apply Yourself
rules and timetables are there to keep you focussed, not to
Punish You
If you're experiencing problems at home, you can
Tell Me
try and see we're here to help you, but first you've got to
Help Yourself

Nana invites Mrs Jayasinha round

There's a soft knocking on Nana's door,
standing there is a small bird
of a woman, cinnamon skin
slight as a feather
wreathed in amber cloth,
wearing a shell necklace.
Come in, come in, says Nana,
she's an eager highland terrier
welcoming her neighbour. She points,
Mother of Pearl we call that, it's a beautiful wee thing.
Thank you, thank you,
Mrs Jayasinha puts her palms together
nods her head
It was given by my mother.
tiny hands hold the shells
up to the window:
See ?
and shows her fingers, dark stripes
through the delicate silver ovals.
Nana's plump tips
touch it gently, I've some china similar,
she reaches into a cupboard, tiptoes
stretches, pulls out her precious
porcelain cup and saucer, with a gold rim,
worn and faded now,
made for dainty tea times long ago.
This belonged to my grandmother.
Nana hands it to the young woman
enjoys the sight of slim wrists
cradling her family treasure.
Mrs Jayasinha lifts it up.
See ? says Nana.
They look at how it holds light,
empty, weightless
yet full of mystery and promise.
They stare, silent,
not knowing what the other really sees.

A fistful of dolers

The lads hang around outside
Sid's corner shop,
Lee's on a bike, his foot on a bollard
like a cowboy in the saddle,
the bike rolls back and forth,
restless as a horse,
Dez and Shabber lean against the wall
one leg bent back, foot on bricks
tabs cupped in hands,
jackets bulge with shapes
carried beneath, out of sight.
Sean stands, hands in pockets
scuffing trainers on the pavement:
the gang, the posse,
the insignificant seven.
Grouped round the door,
loitering, muttering,
putting off shoppers
irritating the shopkeeper
waiting,
waiting for their lives
to happen.

Lee

Always been tall fer his age
can get away wi murder,
his Mam says.
He's loose, but ready
wired like a whippet
in the trap
his head droops forward
his black cap a sleek snout
peak down
so no-on sees his invisible eyes,
but he's always sniffing around
looking out
for the main chance;
he's lived on his wits since he was thirteen
when he became the man of the house,
the breadwinner, the minder:
Don't take shit
Don't trust anyone
Get the first punch in.

Lee's Mam

is a hot chilli pepper
that's seen better days,
wrinkled red skin
hands scratch, her fingertips
bitten to the quick are blood-specked,
she picks at chipped varnish, face and skin
like peeling paper, fiddling, edgy
laughing. She's too thin
her skirt is short,
her legs are bare,
a tab never out of her mouth
feet never still,
trace a stain on the carpet.

The lads troop in, she smiles, they
sit about. She offers tea, but has no milk.
Ignores what's going on over her sitting room floor.
Brown squares, white powder, blue pills and cans of lager,
Lee, handing out the fiver deals.

She limps, an accident on stairs,
I was drunk, six stone, my hip broke:
Lee's Dad sectioned me, then did off, she laughs,
asks to borrow money.
Aye, ok. I got yer tea, ma, it's chop suey.
Yer good ter me, son.
Aye Ma.
Lee stuffs a tenner into her pocket
full of tabs, matches, cough mixture,
a beer mat with a telephone number on it.
She pulls prescription pills out like sweets,
swigs a couple with a nip from a flask.
I'm much better, she says, I'm gettin a job soon.
Aye Ma, he says, I'm off out.

Stone

Hoo hoo hoo, Eee Eee
Lee's doing a chimpanzee
he bares his teeth
at the Jayasinha's boy
the other lads laugh, cheer
him on.
The boy ignores them
his face set in stone,
annoyed they goad and shout
their faces twisted into grins
their shoulders hang
their hands wave
like infuriated animals
in a cage, copying each other
until Lee picks up a rock
throws it - in shock
the lads laugh
and slope away.

Mrs Jayasinha washes up

I am singing this day, a lullaby
my mother sang to me
I am washing my dishes
looking out of my kitchen window
bushes with flowers, pink and blue
many tiny petals, but together
as big as a child's soft head.
My lady neighbour tells me:
Hydrangea. Hydrangea.
I practise this word
the colours remind me of Home, but
there is beauty in this country too
and I sing.
Then I hear running feet
my heart beats, it's my son
his face is washed
like my dishes, there is blood
on his forehead, a small cut
but it hurts deep in me.
He does not weep,
he points and says
These teenage boys:
one shouts at me
Go Back Home Paki !
one throws a stone.

I say Why can't they leave us alone ?
I want to hold my son
and never let him go, but he pulls away
with tiger eyes he looks at me:
Don't Tell Papa.

Nana talks to Brian at the Community Centre about Grandad

He worked in the shipyards all his life
neat as a golfer, but his hands were big as crane hooks
ye could see they wiz powerful tools
one tip on his ring finger missing.
He was fierce and unafraid, and he loved his work.
He'd take me and thi grandbairns to the museum,
Now this's a turbine
with a single flow triple compound
with a dummy piston, shunt-wound
the blading is formed from a delta metal strip
gashed on the skew.

He made me laugh, I couldne understand a word,
He said the same about me, when we first met.
He called me Jock. I felt so different at first,
he made me feel I belonged.

Aye, he loved thi museum, thi working machinery
they were both from another century, there's few
left who remember it.
He used to tease thi grand bairns
tell them Grandad speaks three languages:
Geordie, English and Bad language.
It was his wee joke,
but they all spoke like that, effing and blinding was normal,
in the Yards.
I miss his wee jokes.
I've too much time now, I need to be busy.
I'd like to help others feel they belong too.
Geordie, Scots, Russian, Iranian, we're all the same really
eh hen ?

Tea time

Mam's dishing out the tea, Shepherd's Pie
her cheeks have two red spots
anxiously she cuts up tomatoes, cucumber
looks up as Dad slides in the door
Wash your hands, I know where
they've been all day.
Bird muck. Kylie set the table.
I'm watching TV.
Mam rattles cutlery,
pushes past Dad slowing soaping his hands.
Kylie flops onto the settee, flashes the handset
flicks through channels speedily
Dad can do it.
I'll just have it on me knee, Dad says and dries his hands.
Where's Sean ? Mam shouts, kicking the oven door
shut with her foot, hair sizzling,
hurrying the hot dish onto the table
she stares, it steams:
I'll just talk to meself then;
she dishes up plates, plates onto trays
silently each take them, oblivious,
Kylie watching Vampire-slaying teenagers
Dad holding up something small between his finger and thumb.
Boody, he announces.
He displays a small piece of china
white with blue patterns, an edge, a chip
a shard of plate he's pulled from the tip
Boody was our money when we were bairns,
playing shops. The better the pattern
the more it was worth. Two shillin' this,
He smiles, Kylie stares, Mam rolls her eyes
I'll bloody boody you in a minute.
She leaves her food, stands at the front door
lights a tab, watches the west turn peachy
tapping her toes, wondering about Sean

where he's gone and those meal times
once upon a time
when they sat round the table
all together.

Down the Dene

five tab ends in the dark
Shabber, Scotty, Lee, Dez and Sean
hustling and bustling
clicking sticks
buzzin and whizzin
jabberin and jokin
rapping and rhyming
throwing out lines:

Coming on strong
with a bucket, and a bong
got the boosh, got the booshwah
got the tack, the weed, the ganj
for a smoke, minna moke
got the dope, got the rope,
got the skins, getting skinned up, way up high
laughing, off it,
getting wrecked, well stoned,
getting chongo, monged
chongofied, chinkified
we're laughing laughing can't stop laughing.
Bushes rustle
stones click
a flick of the head
jumpin, on a skitz
the bizzies are buzzin
round the dene
it's the pigs, the polis,
radios jabber
lads all scatter
gotta Nash, gotta dash
coke bottles, plastic,
ripped Rizla packets
lighters, grass
everything trampled
only footprints
left.

Kylie's night out

She's wearing her pink top
with lacy straps, it's stretched
round her slim body,
her belly pouts like a mouth
her jeans show the top of her hips
A zip so short it's hardly there !
tuts Mam, You're getting
undressed to go out.
Kylie says nowt, but lines her lips
and checks her reflection: gold at her lobes
chains round her neck.   Grabs her bag and she's gone
to the Blue Diz-zee - Scotty is MC
tonight.
Meets Sammi, Dawn, Debbie and Jo
at the Metro. They share a tab
then heel it out as the yellow train
opens its doors, the buzzer sounds:
she's away, up, high, zipping over Byker
looking down on her childhood as the sun sets
leaving fifteen behind, she's eighteen
for tonight.

Will he notice her, call her name out
give her a shout while he's on the mike ?
Is this the night,
tonight ?

Scotty does his MC thing

Checka check it out now
time to score
gange and cowie
time to soar
out the window
time to fly
poppin an' a rockin
gettin   high

bidda bidda bad boys
on a roll
goin fasta
outta control
minna minna
movin to the beat
MCMaster
lift your feet

didda didda dancin
Blue Diz-zee
After Dark
buzzin on Ee
MC Master
gotta new sound
gotta stash, gonna crash
passin it round

MCMaster
never get caught
bidda betta listen
you won't get taught
bidda bidda bad boys
on the town
crashing and nashing
get on down

The chill out room

Purple sofas, blue lighting
bottles of water and glistening bodies
scattered like the tide's gone out.
It's 2 am; Sammi and Kylie
are having a breather from heaving dancers
the relentless beat. Sammi spies him
digs her elbow into Kylie's ribs.
Look who's here, eh ?

Across the room Scotty stands
tall and skinny in a peaked cap
and stripy top.   He turns
Kylie raises her hand, just a little
he moves slowly, fast : Hi Kylie
Hiya
Enjoying the sound ?
Aye.   Scotty ?
Aye ?
Will yer give us a shout out on the mike, next time.
Will yer ?
Aye. Ok

As they push back onto the dance floor
crowded as a swimming pool
above the bass 'n drums, the driving rhythm
they hear:
Coming on Strong
It's MC Master
rock your bodies to the beat
c'mon people, move those feet
Hold tight Kylie, and the Byker Massive !
pump it up, drive it up
up to the very top

but all Kylie hears is the echo of her name
ringing in her ears.

Mam thinks about Dad

I worry, I can't help it
I cannot sleep till I hear
the door go, then I know
Kylie's back. God knows
where Sean gets to. And him:
we lie there, not speaking
his back like the Roman Wall
endlessly silent,
but crumbling; our bed bleak
as a Northumberland winter.

When he does talk
it's a different language,
he might as well be an Emperor from Gaul.
I tell him he's useless as a brick;
like a Roman Mile, he's odd
a bit short
nobody needs him anymore.

I spose I should feel sympathy;
it breaks a man to lose his job,
those foreign companies acting like gods
taking over, they divvent care,
don't take account
of what it does to the families.

With a pigeon in his hand
he comes alive;
the way he parts the feathers
with such care, and puts his lips
to that warm breast
like once he did to me.
To think how I used to race to his arms
my heart flying.

Mam's dream

When I do sleep, I dream
of how it was, how it might have been
that summer in 1984,
when the world turned upside down.

The Raby, afternoon
sun slants in through
stained glass windows
making a weedy light
like we're underwater
my brother and his pal Jack
half in shadow, talking low
there's a quiet hum of voices
the clink of glasses
the smell of leather seats
and Golden Virginia - Jack
rolls his own.   There's
an air of defeat, they stare
at me, holding their brown pints
nearly empty, laced with froth.
My brother says, I'm emigrating, lass.
To Australia - start a new life.
There's nowt here for us,
he looks into his glass
Then Jack says, Aye, real slow
An I'm gannin too.

And I wake with the sun on my face
I turn and look at my life
feel the stone in my chest.

The Bella Brigade meet the lads in the park

Down the pavilion a fashion parade
posing on the steps, the Bella Brigade

lads in the bushes, a breeze block party
faces like dishpans, kecks all clarty

a tipple in the rubble is a can of red bull
lasses sup Lambrusco, waitin for a pull

alcopops, wkd, cherryade and vodka
squawkin, larkin, a slab of Lambrella

the dene is spinnin, Shabber hoys a whitey:
Soz Dez, soz, Dez says, Aye Shite, ye !

they're all laughin, its a sick joke.
Gan on, Sean son, gorra tab, gorra smoke?

Scotty eyeing Kylie, she feels his stare
he moans Nee money, nee more beer.

Girls are gigglin, shoving together
Scotty is laughin, movin nearer

Kylie and Scotty, sittin and moochin
eyes on each other, holding hands and snoggin

Kylie smiling wide as the sky
Scotty winks at Sean, who shouts, That's sly

that is. Sean is ugly, starts to makes a scene
Kylie gets angry, stands in-between them

Come on Scotty, let's gan forra walk.
Arm in arm they go off in the dark.

Kylie's carrying Nana's shopping

I always think
we're seeing thi same river and sky
thi first Romans saw, then thi keelmen,
thi soldiers, thi sailors and miners,
thi teddy boys and now you disco lasses.

Nana, yer don't call it disco lasses.

Standing on thi station
of Byker Metro thi other day
watching a couple kiss
I was reminded of the War.

What was it like, Nana ?

Wartime was like a railway line
curving away out of sight,
none of us knew our destinations.
Men were always saying goodbye
on railway platforms. Coming or going
it wis a good excuse for a squeeze, anyways,
hugging under great coats
feelin hot, despite thi freezin wind
thi end of a weekend
maybe thi end.
It made us restless,
we thought we'd invented sex.
That wis before I met your grandad, mind.

The coat

Nana sighs, knows it's time
to face the task
sort the past, his shirts
and shoes, hat and trousers.

Opening the cupboard, the coat
shocks her. It's him, waiting
to be gathered in her arms
smelling of engine oil, allotment air.

Burying her head in it, she cries
his name, unexpected tears,
whispers her fears for the family
he's left behind, his heirs

to an uncertain future; then holds
the coat at arms length
flicks dust, admires its cut
remembers the life left in it.

She needs all her strength
to put it in the bin bag.

Scotty gets dizzy

The lads are hanging out at Lee's,
lounging on his Mam's settee
watching footy on tv,
cans of Fosters, bottles of coke
and all the lads are having a smoke.
Bad boy Scotty's up a height,
mixin it, messin it, talkin shite:
Shabber disses my decks
I'm gonna smack'm
that's pure shady, proper stimnady
proper slobber, Shabber,
don't go dissin me, dosser
tosser, skip rat
ye cannot scratch my vinyl,
hard core, trance or fast dance.
Nee stottin ye.
Shabber's prodding Scotty
Did yer shag her yet ?
Dez says, Have yer ?
Lee says, I would, me,
Gan on, give her one, give her three
Gan on Scotty man, get yer end away
Now's yer big chance, she fancies ye.

They pass round the spliff, some more cans of lager
Scotty takes a swig
he's acting Mr Big
he grabs Shabber
shaking, he's blabberin
on about nooky, sayin:
Aye, I'm gonna buck her the neet,
she's a slag, a grubber,
gonna buck her,
good and proper,
she'll babble then she'll bubble
I divvent give a monkey's.
Mint me, cushtie, lush
I'm flying, belter.

Kylie dreams

In a dream of What Ifs
she stares out her window
across the night view
over the Wall, the balconies
the trees and scrubby bushes
the spire of St Michael's
down to the quayside
where the posh footballer's flats
have pride of place, twinkling
lit up turquoise, purple, electric blue.

Her and Scotty in a love nest
in the air, smart, in the heart
of the city. Later maybe
a baby or two, but first
a job, perhaps in travel
or the perfume counter
of Fenwicks, curvy glass bottles
golden liquid
shiny labels:
Opium, Chanel, Calvin Klein
giving make-up advice
to footballer's wives. Her dream
is cut short by a shout –
'Kyleee !
Scotty's outside
calling up to her,
she leans over the balcony
her hair flowing
and drops down the keys.

In the dark, fumbling

with fingers, lips and thumbs
it's hard to tell what's what
It's like I'm two people:
being me and watching me,
wanting to and feeling No,
Scotty kissin an kissin me,
puttin his hand
up here, down there
this hot wave creepin from below.
Me face's burning but I'm ice
feeling odd, it's not right.
He's drunk and stoned
I want to push him away
but I'm holding tight.
Wonderin what it'll be like

I smell the tabs on his breath
I feel sick to me stomach
but I can't tell him to go
will it be ok ? I want to know
Does he love me ? Will he afterwards ?

I stare, he lights a tab,
says, You alright ?
he strokes me hair
I cannot stop the tears,
I whisper, Scotty ? Do yer love me ?
he says nowt but It's late,
like he didn't hear me and I
don't ask again.

Nana does Asylum Seekers Morning

at the Community Centre
outside
is like a high security prison
cameras on poles, high wire fences
no windows, heavy padlocks on the doors
concrete garden, no grass
a touch of graffiti the only splash of colour
in this grey place.

Inside
is warmth and smiles from Brian Y'alreet ?
Nana and the local women share tea bags
between three cups and laugh as they sort
black plastic bin bags of clothes, books
shoes and bric-a-brac.
At ten o'clock the world arrives:
Mongolians, Malaysians,
Romanians, Serbians,
Africans, Czechoslovakians, all
without a space, aliens
living in the Wall
seeking asylum, needing
anything
as they left
everything
behind.

There's racks of jumpers, T shirts, sweat shirts
tops and joggers, dresses, pyjamas
knickers and socks and bibs and bits and bobs.
Buggies, books, plates and cutlery
sofas and suites, curtains and help
with the jigsaw puzzle of filling in forms.

The coat finds a new home

Brian brings in a new face
Nana sees it's the man from number 56
she holds out her hand, he takes it
his slim brown fingers feel cold
are bone to her warm skin.

Good Morning. I am Mr. Jayasinha.
Greetins, I'm Aggie.
I've met yer wee wife, we're neighbours.
he nods, his face grave
his eyes have a spark
that ignites her into action
Yer jacket isne thick enough.
Excuse Me ? he's trying to translate
It's cold - brr - whit ye need's a guid coat,
without a moment's hesitation
she pulls it from the bag
and both of them are smiling
as he puts it on.

The Centre Committee

Brian pulls them in
for a planning session;
what to do about
the refugees
and the complaints that the council
won't lift a finger.
They've had this discussion
a hundred times before:
Doris is firm. We need to beat crime and fear.
the vicar says, We need to pull the estate together.

Brian suggests an event
a celebration for all the residents,
Nana says, Whit aboot a wee Pot Luck dinner ?
Mrs Haq from the council agrees
says she'll provide publicity.
Nana says she'll ask Mrs Jayasinha
to contribute a dish.
Brian is pleased
with this small success.

Nana talks to Sean

When I was a wee lassie we had goats
it was my job to milk them. Up at five every day.
Allotments and domestic animals,
you don't see them so much now.
They've gone, like the jobs,
the apprenticeships, all those lovely wee boys
goin off with their bait every morning
spring in their step, to a real job.
Now ye just sign on, or eat paper in the Civic, if you're
lucky,
or talk all day in a call centre.
I mean, whit sort of job is that ?
To me, that's no usin yer muscle or yer mind,
no challenge to it.

There's nee jobs that'll have me, anyways, Nana.

I see you young lads, sittin on the walls
all skin and bone. No difference between ye
and the wrecks of old cars.
It breaks my heart to see it,
going to waste.

I like hanging out with the lads, they're me mates.

Having something to do
keeps me going, Sean.
Helps me get out of bed every morning.

I'm not bothered.

It might help you.

Aye, Nana, divvent gan on.

Multi cultural lunch at the Centre

Mrs Jayasinha is a bird of paradise
in floaty layers of startling pink and orange
tinkling with bangles
she moves on feet that never touch the earth
her hands flutter like wings

she lays out dishes of delicate scent
fluffy rice, golden stews
smiling with her face, her eyes uncertain
can this really be true ?
Grinning Nana has an apron on,
spooning stew onto paper plates.
Mrs Haq is confident in her turquoise salwar kameez
at ease in these situations, she welcomes
the small crowd generously:
the vicar, the luncheon club from the day centre
Brian and a handful of Refugees.

Mrs Jayasinha sings her song,
her husband holds her steady with his eyes,
three Iranian musicians play a dance tune
the luncheon club clap along.
Brian sings an Irish lament he knows
then Betty with a good voice is urged
to sing her usual, hits from the shows.
The afternoon ends in a medley:
Pack up Your Troubles, We'll Meet Again
and cups of tea.

Teen Talk

Haway Kylie !
Sammi calls for me,
says, It's chilly out.
windows in the Wall like eyes
watching us
the bushes and litter bins
look different
like strange dogs
or crouching people.
It's Teen Talk tonight
I'm not keen,
Sammi's blabbing on
about a skirt she's seen
in Top Shop.
We stop at the door,
for a tab
our usual, we light up
Sammi looks young,
I feel old,
the sky is violet,
we stamp our feet
I take two drags
stub it out
head feels big like an empty balloon
Sammi, I says
Aye ?
Nothing.
And we go in.

It's about Safe Sex
I sit, say nowt
while this wifey gans on
showing pictures of positions
waving this condom
all the others giggle
all except me.

Getting up

The alarm goes off at seven thirty
Kylie feels as tired as death
like she hasn't slept
her legs and arms are made of lead
she cannot lift them off the bed

she hears Mam shouting
Tea's in the pot.
then
C'mon Kylie, it's nearly eight o'clock.

Kylie lies still, unable to move
the light grows stronger through
a crack in the curtains. Kylie is certain
if she sits up now
her head will fall off.

Eight fifteen, Mam bursts in
For God's sake Kylie, yer'll be late
an it's me that'll get into trouble.
Kylie whispers from the duvet
I don't feel great.
Mam scoffs, Yer can't fool me.

Kylie opens her mouth to speak
but her stomach flips
like a skipping rope
she leaps out of bed
locks the door of the toilet
and heaves, cold sweat on her brow.

Mam sighs,
I'll phone school then.

Mrs Jayasinha does her shopping

I am carrying my shopping.
Through the bushes I see these boys and men
many of them, standing in my path.
They are holding big sticks.
Brian tells me these are for a game,
to me they are just big sticks.
They do not see me
but there is no other way to my house
I think I will turn around
go to Brian at the Centre, wait there
wait for them to go.
One of them has a small dog, it is strong
pulling at its rope, it is sniffing and growling
at me, showing teeth
the boys and men turn, see me
sniff and growl and show their teeth
like dogs,
their words - I don't understand
except Paki Cow.
My legs are young trees in wind
inside I am water, like sea leaving the beach
my mouth is dry sand.
But I think of my son coming home from school
I think of my husband, what would he do ?
I hold my head up
I sing words in my head
I look up - I do not see boys
I see my mother, other men holding guns
and I remember why I am here
so I walk.
They push me and pull my scarf
I am walking through a forest of hands
an army of bad words
but they let me pass.
I get home. I am sick
in the kitchen sink.

Messages for Kylie

Text :
We R in Pk
C U ?
Sammi

Ansaphone :
Er...aye....hi
it's me....Scotty
er...you're not in...
I'll ring....later
bye

A scrap of paper on the table :
Kylie, I'm out with Nana
pizza in fridge
pop it in 4.30
back at five
Mam

The mess in the kitchen :
says Sean was here
and muddy footprints
leading to the sitting room
says Dad's in there.

Kylie wants a talk with Dad

Dad, have yer ever thought, like, if things were different
what would you be ?

I sometimes wonder what it would be like
to be a pigeon

Aye - think with a pigeon's eye
seeing one grain on the dusty floor

the wicker basket, fretting the light
the feel of other pigeons warm and close

large hands reaching towards you
holding your wings firm

a blinding light as yer set free
then all of the country laid out below.

I sometimes think the Byker Wall
is like a big pigeon cree

all them nesting humans, ruffling their feathers
one on top of the other in their little cages

callin to each other, billing and cooing
beady eyes at the small windows

feeling the light, watching the horizon
waiting for the right moment

to launch themselves out
into the world, to escape.

Bloody pigeons !
Is that all yer ever think about, Dad ?

Kylie won't talk to Mam

She pulls her red striped Nike top
and fumbles with the zip
she's feeling useless, queasy,
nothing's easy
these days.

From her window
she can see the football stadium
like a white castle, she can hear them roar
Sean and Scotty are at the match,
kings of the league
as white turns to gold
in the autumn sun,
she can see the river, glinting like a knife.

She touches her Westlife poster, ripped at the edge
her pink hairbrush, tangled with blonde
her tv, her cd, then her stomach, it aches.
This doesn't add up to a life.

Lying on her bed
staring at the wall
lying to herself about dates and signs
remembering girls behind ringed fingers
whispering old wifies tales:
not on your first time, not standing up,
not if you didn't come, not if it's your period.

A careful tock tock !
sets her face to a closed door
it's Mam's knock,

Kylie ? Kyle ? Canna come in ?
Her dressing gown trembles on the peg
as the handle turns.
She stand at the glass
her back the only part of herself she trusts.
Are yer alreet pet ?
She shrugs
Yer seem very quiet, like.
So ?
Ye've not touched yer tea.
Silence
A made chips.
Leave us alone.
In the mirror
she catches Mam
looking back at her
with a face shaped into a question
she doesn't want her to ask.
She holds her breath and waits.
Mam gives up, she breathes out,
the door shuts, a tear escapes
the quiet evening closes in
like a million feathers fluttering down
smothering her, each one a word she wishes
she'd uttered to her mother.

White

The white lid
of the toilet
sticks to her legs
as she waits
making white rings
on her thighs
it's the only room
that locks
even though
she's the only one
in the flat;
the frosted glass
lets in
a hazy white light
she can hear her wrist
watch, its tiny white ticks
and her blood
in her ears,
the white water rushing
in the pipes upstairs
the white noise
of the central heating
and her own
shallow breathing
white faced
as she watches the line
in the middle
of the white stick
change colour.

Hoying up

I couldn't wait, just hoyed up
all down the wheels of this blue van
didn't make the toilets,
they stink anyways, locked
cos the lads hang out, sniff glue
and drink and that.
Just leant on the bonnet, chucked up
could see me breakfast, toast and tea
all brown and bitty
couldn't get the taste out me mouth
had to go to school, I'd promised Mam.

The Welfare wifey was waitin
face like a cat's arse, all frowny lines
lookin at her watch, dead obvious like.
I wanted to shout, Leave us be,
I'm hoyin me guts up
an all ye want is me name in the register
before the bell goes !
I'm here ent I ?
is all I says.
I feel like death warmed up
goin to hoy up again
so I keep me mouth tight
say nowt. Nowt, right.

Not givin them the pleasure
I know what they'll say
if word gets out
be all over, man. Nah.
Keep me mouth shut
swallow it
down.

Mr Jayasinha speaks

In the hall the silence is complete
all eyes watch and wait for this newcomer
resentment hovers as Mr J's voice
skates out over thin ice:

My country is very beautiful.
The blue of the sea is like a jewel
the sand is white,
there are palm trees, tall as your buildings
fresh coconut, and flowers pink like sunrise.
And you might ask me
Why leave such a beautiful country ?

And I would tell you
my country is also very poor;
poverty makes people bad.
You must pay this man
to get your passport
and that man
for your ticket for the train.
You must pay the men
or the soldiers come
to your door and say,
Your papers are not in order.
They lock you up
and even if you can pay,
sometimes they will not let you out.

Friends helped us to escape,
to come to Britain. This would not happen here.
You are lucky people.
We are grateful for your country's freedoms.

And I ask you, since you are lucky,
will you not also be generous ?

Dad speaks out

Generous ? Generous ?
Our industries failed because of countries like yours.

The far east could build ships cheaper
because they paid your lot slave wages

your slave wages meant I lost mine.
What about that then ?

And if there's nee work fer us here,
they'll be even less for you, bonny lad.

And the hall bursts into a hundred different
conversations,
accusations,
consternation.
Nana turns in her chair,
Brian runs his fingers over his head
and despairs.

Kylie visits Nana

Kylie trails though the walkways
trying to finish her tab
before she arrives at her Nana's
past peeling paint and drab
litter-strewn gardens.

Once these houses were bright
green, blue and red
now windows are boarded up
a lot of the old community are dead
and young ones move away.

Nana has seen all the changes
says she'll never leave
she sees good in everything
Yer have to believe, hen
expect the best, and nine times out of ten ye'll get it.

A bitter wind shakes the trees
she hears a sudden dog bark
Kylie hurries to Nana's front door
Come in, hen. It's getting dark
out there. Will you have a cup o tea ?

The small kitchen smells of cake
the evening news trickles from the radio
Nana's world is safe and timeless
Kylie sits and feels she's letting go
of something very heavy, held too long.

Nana takes the teapot down to make a brew
watching Kylie from the corner of her eye
she puts the knitted cosy on the pot
settles in her chair: Now tell me.
Whit's the news ?

Kylie talks to Nana

Y'kna like..
y'get this feelin
when something's
happened
an you don't, y'na like
know what to do ?
Something's
happened
to me, like, and I
don't know what to do
y'na like
what I mean ?

As she walks home
Kylie thinks the good thing
about Nana's way of talking
is the space she leaves for you
a helpful quiet
not a stony place
big enough to swim around and reach
your own conclusions
no-one shouting, pushing you
in this or that direction.
She hasn't told Nana everything
but wonders if she's guessed
as if the look in Nana's eyes
has guided her, made her realise
she feels less depressed
now she knows she's going to tell her parents
get if off her chest.

The Jayasinha family

At seven o'clock, it is calm. A hint of spice
tinges the air: ginger, garlic, star anise;
they sit with plates on knees
in front of the tv
the three of them, on their second-hand sofa
the faded pattern threadbare,
the one lamp lights them to a burnished brown
the sound is turned down,
they are reading the subtitles in English for practice
the gas fire hisses.

The peace is shattered
by a battered front door, three lads roar in
looking, touching, shouting, nicking
Mr Jayasinha grabs his wife
who pulls their son behind them both,
she is crying Who ? and Why ?
their boy stares with frightened eyes
at his father, afraid of what he might do.
Mr Jayasinha is still and firm.
I call Police. They arrest you.

Sean is red-eyed, laughs out loud
convinced he's invincible
I divvent give a shite, giz yer money.
I have nothing.
Sean kicks the wall, blasting a hole in the thin plaster
angry at the world.
Grabbing a coat, he runs into the dark
followed by his mates, heading for the park,
leaving the lock broken on the family's door
and their world falling apart.

The stolen coat

The lamps are broken, there's a cloudy moon
the stolen coat throws a mud-stained arm
out from under the bush, half-hidden
like a badly kept secret, Kylie screams
she sees blood, a body, imagination
running away with her down the dark footpath.

Clifford Street police station
a constable filling in forms, asking questions
Mr Jayasinha answers in halting English
hating his lack of accuracy, he wants
to be precise,
A coat, he says
My coat. They take it.
The constable wants details
colour, size and value
doesn't understand the coat
is the least of it.

Round at Scotty's, Sean is boasting
about paper-thin doors and flimsy people,
Fockin sweet - just walk in
off the street, kick the door
they don't say nowt - we took
owt we liked, a useless coat
an old tv, a stupid picture. Pakis, man,
pathetic, pissin themselves.
Haven't even got owt to pinch,
to score I'll have to go back
try next door.

Sean gets arrested

Convinced she's just witnessed a body that's dead
dashing past bushes, the scene in her head,
running and breathing so hard she feels sick
a sight through the archway brings her up quick:

neighbours are out to watch the commotion
spotlights are pinpointing Sean's wild emotion.
A copter above, whirring over the scene
is strobing Sean's body, he's making obscene

gestures, he's high as a kite on a string
everyone's shouting and pointing at him
up on a balcony, he's waving his arms
cursing the polis, the siren's alarms.

Pushing through people, she reaches her Dad
scratching his head, says, I think Sean's gone mad.
Mam is cajoling through a red megaphone
Sean's got a spliff, he shouts, Leave us alone !

Kylie is green, she throws up in a rush
Dad sighs, Oh dear, disappears in the crush,
Mam keeps on talking, she's watching Sean's eyes
which don't see the polis catch him by surprise.

How many walls make right ?

Sean's banged up in a cell all night
four tiled walls and a shadeless light

the family he harassed have left their flat
no walls at all, afraid to go back.

Sean's Statement to the Police

I'm not sayin nowt til me solicitor gets here

What Sean said to his solicitor

Me last can of Fosters was in the bin,
there were no pills left to pop
me an the lads were out of tabs
no cash left to gan t'the shops

me and Shabber were on a come down
from a blaster yesterday neet
I was proper chokin
for a good smoke 'n
I was so tired I couldn't stand on me feet

me hands were shakin, me mouth was puar skankin
says Lee, I'll give yer some EEs
but I need more cash
to buy a stash
so you lot'll have to help me

I was off me heed, I was on a skitz
we din't knaa what we was deein
and Lee says Haway, it's easy as owt
I din't kna he would spark im

we went to this house, Lee's shouting gan on
so I kicks in the door with one blow
there was this gadgy standing so still
with his wife and his lad, I dunno

what I was thinking, I can't really remember
what I did

The Row

Oh my god !
Sean, what are you like
ye've gone too far this time

Don't kick off, Ma !
It wasn't me
I never meant ter do it

Yer beyond control
I'm sick of yer
It's them Ee's yer taking
Look at him !
Look at yer son!
Have ye got nowt to say ?

Well, I don't know

In front of the neighbours
Any trouble now
the polis call here first

Your Ma's right

It's Sean this
and Sean that
and then it's Sean the other

They made us do it
It wasn't me
it was Shabber, and Lee

Haway, divvent lie to me
I kna what's what
Yer've gone & done it this time

Stop shouting
Yer violent !
Robbin poor folk !
You'll have us all in trouble

I didn't take much,
all fockin rubbish.
They're only pakis, man

Bad Language
Bad behaviour
the polis'll have you for this

What did yer do Sean ?

I never touched him
the polis are lyin
I only took a coat

Tell him Dad

Don't keep shouting !

Oh, I don't know

If you were the man
my father was
we wouldn't have this trouble.

Don't start on that.

For fock's sake !
It's just a paki's coat
Alright ?

Later

I hate it
when they shout
all that shoutin
does my head in.

When Mam and Dad argue
like poison in the air
spreading everywhere,

when Sean gets wrong
everyone's up a height
boilin forra fight

because I wanted a quiet night
so's I could get it right
when I tellt them.

But they went ballistic
and I missed it,
my chance,
so I said nowt.

Nana gives Sean a talking to

Did yer know the Byker Wall lies
along the line of an older, Roman one ?
Listen, hen, just imagine the Romans
invaded your home, right now, kicked thi door, marched in.
Powerful folk, wi masses of soldiers, weapons, armour.

You'd get angry, upset would'n ye ? Aye.
so you'd try and stand up to them,
but they kill or arrest folk like you.
Now you're in trouble. They've got your number, son.

You have to leave, without delay
just walk away, dressed like that
no time to pack a bag, no money.
Have you a passport ? No - I thought not.

Imagine, no more tea on the table,
no comfy bed, no knowing if
your Mam or Dad are dead,
afraid to trust yer neighbours.
Where will you go ?
Who will protect ye ?
Now imagine that family you robbed,
that's whit happened to them.
They're not Roman, no, nor from Pakistan, neither.
You don't know where they're from, do ye ?

Ye don't know whit they're like, do ye ?
I'll tell ye - the father's a teacher
the Mam owned a wee shop
and all they want
is for their son to get an education
to find a happy life.
Because they've no job, no property.
Not so very different from your ma and da, eh ?

Just imagine the Refugee families round here
could be your uncles, cousins, brothers.
Because they are.

A coach trip to Vindolanda

Dawn kicks her bag closer to Kylie's
hisses Miss'll go ballistic if she sees
them earrings. A bubble smacks
Want a hubba bubba ?
Kylie unwraps the pink square and chews
sweetness stifling her need to spew.
Ten girls, ten packed lunches and coats
in case of weather, wait between brick wall
and coach, Dawn grumbles Why can't we get on ?
School trips; what a pain. Who wants
to see a stupid wall anyhow ?
The others mutter, Kylie is silent
her eyes look away, distant as clouds
that threaten rain.
Miss Hood the history teacher urges
Come along girls, you're the lucky ones
chosen to visit this world heritage site.
Dawn whispers, world heritage shite
a giggle ripples through the group.
Who knows who built Hadrian's Wall ?
The Vikings ? No.
President Kennedy ? Miss Hood sighs.
Hadrian ? ventures Kylie, Miss Hood is surprised
I didn't think you were listening. Yes
and what was he ? A brickie
quips Dawn and everyone laughs
the coach trip is on its way.

Kylie watches out the window
a film of countryside stream past:
rich rusty bracken, autumn sun
a light breeze, trees freeze framed,
a hot air balloon
hanging like a plump ripe fig.

At Vindolanda, ten pairs of shoes shuffle
into the dim-lit small museum,
Miss Hood is telling them: These
are the earliest writings recorded,
The Vindolanda Tablets.
Take two, yawns Dawn, for boredom.
Tantalising fragments of domestic and military life;
short messages sent back and forth across the empire:-
come to my birthday party, send more socks.
Kylie stares at the display, her thoughts
stray : Like Postcards.
Yes ! beams Miss Hood, Exactly like.
And ten girls flap out into the breezy day
thinking who they'd like to send a postcard to
and what they'd say.

Dawn and Kylie, backs against the roman stones
eat their packed lunch, cheesy sticks and snack-a-jacks
coats done up and shoulders hunched
sheltering from the nipping wind.
Dawn says, I'd send a card
to me Dad. I've never seen him
since I was three, and she stares
into her lap, But yer can't post cards
to the past.

Then Kylie blurts it out: My postcard
is to the future -
Dawn turns her head and screws her eyes
tries to read this strange face-
To my baby.
Meet you next May,
on your birthday
safe journey. Love K.

Ee, Kylie, does yer Mam know ?
Kylie shakes her head
and starts to cry.

What Scotty's neighbours hear

The TV constantly - just too loud
the scratching of vinyl and a heavy beat
loud mouthed lads shouting their raps.
Rarely Scotty's Mam, she's a little lamb.

A telephone ringing, a door slam
Scotty's Dad singing his football chants
the clank of empties in the hollow bin
a mother calling her little ones in.

Sometimes, voices
loud scratchy shouting
a bang, a clank, a scream
silence
then quiet weeping.

On Saturday afternoon, Scotty's Dad

is done in after a week at work
wears a vest and holds a can of stella
has a blue-black tattoo creeping round
his arm and neck. He's missing a tooth
and missing his football on tv while Scotty's Mam
is creeping round, trying to tell him
without tripping the wire, something
careful, choosing words, too slow
for him, who slams his hand
down on his knee:
What the fock's he done ?
What ? What !?
he doesn't really want to know
but knows he's got to
act the man, make a stand, draw the line.

Scotty's in his bedroom
listening through the wall
for the sounds that tell him
the news; Dad's on a radge
bawling his rage, Scot !
C'm here yer toe-rag
yer little piece of no-good shite,
what's this ? Who is she ?
I want to hear it from youse -
yer Ma's tellt us aboot this lass.
Well ? Is it true ?

Yeah, but lissen Dad –
Don't you lissen Dad me, lad.
How d'ye kna it's yours ?
Them lasses from the top end Wall
all slags and whores
everyone kna's what's what.

No, Dad, no, she's not like that.
Ye kna nowt, lad
we'll gan there noo and sort it oot.
He stands curling his hands into fists
straightening his knees, lifting
his shoulders with a deep breath.
Wait, Dad.
But Scotty's arm is in his grip,
the door slams and off they march
Scotty, Scotty's Dad, leaving behind
Scotty's Mam, tight faced.
Through the archways
down the path
nets lifting, kids stop playing
everyone senses something brewing;
a small crowd gathers at a distance
as these two stop at Kylie's place
knocking on and on, insistent
Scotty's Dad set with a concrete face.

Kylie's Dad looks with mild surprise
at this unexpected visit,
not prepared for confrontation
he's drinking tea and there are biscuit
crumbs around his mouth, he smiles
and waits. Scotty's Dad gets in there sharp:

Scot says your lass is pregnant. That's a shame
but your lass says it's our Scotty who's to blame,
how'd you kna whose bairn it is ?
She hangs oot with lots of lads
the gang that gather in the park
who knas what gans on after dark ?
If she has it, I'm tellin yer noo
Scotty's having nowt te di with it.
What your lass does, is up ter you
but Scot's too young ter be a Dad
he's got nee money, our lad's not able
to support a bairn. I've tellt him
he's not seeing your lass again.

Kylie's Dad is silent, rocked to the core.
Now Kylie and her Mam are at the door
weak with shock, caught off guard
Mam examines Kylie's face
see's her shifting look, and like a book
she's reading, the last few chapters fall into place.

Eruption

There's a silence, a moment
where time is suspended
far overhead a plane cruises
a metro rumbles
there's a distant hum of traffic
and one car horn blasts.
No-one speaks, but Scotty
shuffles his feet, his Dad
now seems lost for words
he's said them all - he's waiting
but he gets no reply
just three pairs of eyes staring
one in shock, one in anger
one in fear;
Reet then, he starts into action
C'mon Scot, and turning swiftly
they disappear.

The door shuts with a tiny click
that breaks the spell
Mam turns, eyes burning
her mane of hair raging round
she roars, stamps her feet
words spurting between gnarled teeth:
Yer little fool, yer bloody little idiot !
she grabs her daughter
shakes her roughly, screaming :
Bloody little bloody fool !
anger greater than her words can say
or body hold, she lashes out
with one big smack.

Kylie's cheek is shocking red
she's wailing, heaving pain
up from her stomach
pouring it out, eyes sodden
mouth half open, nose streaming
coming apart like paper in rain.

Dad is weeping silent tears
for his little pigeon;
he wants to coo and rock her
make it better, like he could
when she came crying
with a grazed knee
but it's too late for sticking plaster.

Mam sits on the sofa, sobbing, head in hands
repeating: I can't cope, first Sean, now this.
Kylie's on the floor, a little heap;
Dad pulls himself together
he's got to get them through
this family disaster:
Let's all have a cup of tea,
eh pet ?

Life's a drag

Sean's on an ASBO
where he's got a new tag

Nana's phoning NACRO
her shoulders sag

Mam takes an ASPRO
lights her fortieth fag

Kylie's on the METRO
someone whispers, Slag

Dad shops at NETTO
with his black and yellow bag

Scotty runs a DISCO
down the Nag's head.

All of them unhappy.

Sean's new tag

No-one can see it
round his ankle,
no-one knows it's there
under his trousers
except
the never-sleeping eye
of the polis.

They know
where he goes
and when
he's under a curfew
in by seven,
invisible walls
keep him confined.

He feels a volcano
building inside
if he opens his mouth
flames will shoot out
burning them all to hell
which is why he has to
go on an Anger Management Course as well.

Graffiti

Through the arch
the writing's on the wall:

Jen loves Edi cos he's geet lush

K4S4eva

Bella Brigade R fit

then

Bitches from Byker
We screw you all
East End Side
TU - PAC slide

Horny bastards, thc Killa Boyz
Notorious Thugs TU-PACs Drugs
Any style
Doggy style
We get on down
in the east side of your town
Byker Girlz R ezee
with ma dick as Hard az
Hard az a brick

Kylie turns away
she's about to be sick.

Kylie talks to Sammi and Dawn

Mam's tired, out of it on pills, can't think straight
all she says is:
What about exams ?
Yer cannot take a bairn te school.
I've got enough on me plate;
I've got a headache.

Dad's in his pigeon cree, day and night
says it's up ter me:
But yer such a bright lass,
don't throw yer life away
you've got options,
not like me
when I was your age.

Yeah, but how do I decide ?
Gettin rid of it's murder. Nah. No way.
Suicide ? I'd rather die.

Givin it away ?
rich folks, big house
somewhere posh,
a nice safe estate ?
Maybe the baby
would have a better life ?
But how - knowing
that your own ma
didn't want yer ?

But I've no place, nee money
Mam and Dad not talkin
Sean's a liability
Scotty not allowed to come near me
I'd have to leave school
no exams
shit
I divvent kna.

What Mrs Jayasinha sees from her window

There is whiteness everywhere
it sparkles on branches, so bright
the roof, the ground
even the air.
I see my husband, treading with care
he's coming up the street, he smiles
his lovely teeth, I wave
his breath is white, it curls and rises.
He is a dragon,
he has saved me from danger
flown me to a new land
away from demons, fire and hell
brought me to this cold white country
where there are no snakes
with men's faces, no devils
in uniform with guns.

Then I see five white men
see my husband slip
or trip, he falls
the men are round him
arms and legs swinging
in silent white slow motion.
I am shouting, but no-one hears
no-one sees but me;
the men disappear like smoke
I run out. On the white ground
I see him broken,
a tiny trickle of red,
and I know there are devils
everywhere.

What Mr Jayasinha sees from his hospital bed

Brian slumped in a plastic chair
one hand rubbing his eyes, sighing
the other holding a mobile
trying to contact people
organise support and after-care.

His wife, tearful, fearful
sitting at his feet
her fingers clasped together
covering her mouth
to catch her sobs.

His son, hands over his ears
to shut out the world
as he stares out the window
watching his first
snow fall.

Identity

Mrs Jayasinha waits in Clifford Street Police Station
her hands are cold
the chairs are stiff
and fixed to the floor
at reception a ringing telephone
sits behind thick glass.   No-one answers.
Posters on the wall
offer warnings; she is silent
Brian is the only living person
inside this hard world
here to help her.

A Policewoman comes in
with Lee's Mam, her blouse has a rip
her mouth is a sewer
of words she's flinging
at the polis, the paki woman, Brian
accusing them all
of messing with her mind.
She raises her arm and totters, Brian leaps up.
The Policewoman grabs her from behind
drags her off to another world.

Mrs Jayasinha waits for the ID parade
although she's afraid
to face the line
wonders if she can
pick out the ones
who attacked
her husband.

Kylie goes for a walk

There's a salty layer of snow
Kylie hugs her coat around
stands in the shelter
of the brick arch, her tab
flickers in the wind
that teases round the corner.

She follows her feet
leaving prints
lonely as a school yard after home time.

She passes Byker Primary
where she was a bright thing
with bobbles in her hair
she remembers
sitting on the maroon carpet
close to teacher's chair
smelling good shoe leather
hearing, Well Done Kylie;
gold stars and that special Mrs Gibson smile
her rewards.

There's The Cabin, the corner shop
where she would buy red liquorice shoe laces
and flying saucers with her pennies,
where she was trusted
with the treat of buying pop
Irn Bru or Dandelion and Burdock
a litre bottle wobbling in her arms
as the liquid slopped. Now it sells
samosas and mango juice as well,
the window's boarded up
looking more closed than open.
Past The Plough that's lost
its letters - it says Ugh
at Byker now. Kylie
remembers persuading
a bigger girl to go in
to get her first tabs
and bottles of Bella.

In the white-board November sky
pigeons flap and criss-cross
making arithmetic squiggles
as jumbled as her thoughts:
Kylie - Baby = what ?
Kylie + Baby = when ?
Kylie - Scotty ÷ Baby = how ?
Like badly done sums
nothing adds up.

She's cold and numb
the snow blows her over Byker Bridge
the buses drumming on the road.
She leans over, picking out the scene
below: the city farm, sheep
like grey spots on white,
goats trashing hay by the gate
of a scrubby field under the viaduct's
brick legs. Up Stepney Bank the smell
hits her, horses, dung and clopping hooves
of the stables. She rode the tiny shetland ponies
in the summer of her childhood
and didn't ever want to grow up.
She still feels five, but nestling
inside her little self
is a smaller one who will call her
Mammy and push her into
the adult world forever.

Kylie visits Nana again

Once again, Kylie trails through the Wall
she smokes a tab but it makes her sick,
thinking maybe a talk with Nana
would help; a little lad waves a stick
at her and shouts: Giz a tab or piss off !

By Nana's porch the hanging baskets are empty
her garden is always carefully weeded,
but a few doors down it's boarded up
Nana says Families who'll stay are what's needed
but thinks you can't blame them for moving away.

She recalls the last time she came to visit:
the drama of the coat and Sean's arrest,
realises the boarded up house is the one
Sean burgled and she becomes distressed;
is she never going to escape ?

Nana opens the door, a smile on her face
giving Kylie a welcoming hug and kiss
Kylie thinks she might start to cry
but simply says: Hi, I've missed yer Nana,
shall I make us a cup of tea ?

It's warm and quiet, there's a photo on the wall
of Kylie, gap-toothed and scruffy Sean,
his arm around her, Grandad snapped it
long ago on a trip to Byker Farm
when she was six and the world was safe.

Her words tumble out. Granda was lovely
good and kind, and funny.
Look at my life - it's in a mess.
I wish I wasn't going to have this baby,
I'm so unhappy. Her tears cascade.

Nana tells her secret

Listen, hen, I'll tell ye a wee story
I've never told anyone before.
It was a warm September, when I turned fourteen
in Aberdeen at the start of the war.
It was a glowing time, wi long shadows
everything glistened in thi granite city
evening sun set afire to windows,
Ma and Da, all the old folks were greetin
worrying about war, but me, youth's audacity
I thought life was jest beginnin.

Rationin, hardships, shortages, call-up
men and boys going to join the Navy
troops, manoeuvres, movement all up
and down, it was hustle and bustle,
more excitement than I'd ever seen
in my fourteen years in Aberdeen.

We didn't go short, we had plenty:
my Da would collect peewits' eggs
little wee brown things, twenty
or so would fill a frying pan
we'd go to the seashore, catch crabs or else
hunt out gulls eggs, fishy and salty,
Ma'd gather seaweed, we called that Delse
we'd eat it wi vinegar; we improvised
and we got by.

It was 1942, half way though the war
I was lukin for williks, on ma oan
when I saw him walkin on the rocky shore
I could tell he wasne from Aberdeen.
Tall, he was, in a navy greatcoat
he was stood, staring across the sea,
as if looking for a boat.
So still like a statue, his face carved wood,
sad but dignified
I'll never forget that sight.

Imagine my surprise to find him
sittin at oor table, in oor
hoose. He was a soviet seaman
shipwrecked into ma lap
billeted they called it. Oh, hen
he was so different from
the rag taggle of menfolk
left in Aberdeen by then.
He smelt of the wind and foreign tobacco
my eyes only reached his top button
where I could see tanned neck. Oh
he turned many a girl's head, aye.
He showed me ma how to cook a rook,
he told me about his hometown Riga
in Latvia on the Baltic Coast
an he taught me some words of Russian;
I loved to hear him talk, each word
a whole new country that I could see :
Archangel, Leningrad
Simferopol, Odessa:
The Soviet Union.
Riga is on the same latitude as Aberdeen,
we were linked by a line around the earth
I thought that was romantic, meant to be.

With him I went into another world,
carried away to where I felt foreign,
I unfurled
I was his flag, and waved
goodbye to the rules of home
I was fearless, and brave.
Then suddenly he was gone.
I felt defeated and alone, but
he left me a little piece
of himself. You know whit a mean ?

Ma and Da were furious wi him
they'd shown him hospitality
he'd taken more. Heartbroken wi me
in straying from the path.
They were strict Presbyterians.

Ma said she couldn't bear me at home,
wanted to shut it out from her mind,
I'd ruin Dad's good name.
Heaven knows there were a few fell like me
but my kind
were sent away.
A distant cousin of me ma's in Byker
said she would have me. I liked her
but Ma said, Never mention it again.
Don't come home til it's all over.
Ma's word was gospel in our hoose.

Because of the bombin and overcrowdin
in Newcastle City, mothers were sent
to a hospital in the country, Gilsland
by a special coach; The Blunderbus
the girls called it
because there were a few of us
unfortunate, unhappy, unmarried.

I had him early one spring morning
and held him just for a moment
masses of dark hair and Latvian eyes
I loved him instantly,
Gregory, I said
like your father, and kissed him once
Dosvidanye. Goodbye.

I never even suckled him.

After Kylie's talked to Nana

Kylie and Nana on the settee
sharing tissues, wiping their eyes

Kylie hugs Nana, she hugs back.
They're both glad they had this talk

Kylie puts the kettle on, looks for Nana's sweets
they sip tea and suck Black Bullets watching Coronation
Street

Nana says I sometimes think of Gregory
and wonder does he wonder about me ?

Ten thirty, Nana makes her cocoa
Kylie goes, walking slowly through the snow.

Christmas is coming

Christmas is coming and Kylie's getting fat
Sean's been refusing to decorate the flat
Dad hasn't got a ha'penny, Mam's feeling blue,
the days are short and dark - what are they to do ?

Season of goodwill

Worst fuckin christmas ever !
Bloody tag.   Like a bloody dog.

What yer gannin on aboot ?

Piss off, Nebby.

Piss off yerself, yer really gettin on my tits, moanin round.

Ye can talk.

You're not the only one wi problems, Sean.

Aye. It's your fault I never see Scotty no more.

Fuck Right off, Sean !

'fuck right off Sean.'

Tell him Ma !

'tell him Ma !'

Quiet both of ye ! Yer givin me a headache.

Give yer Ma some peace, eh ?
And don't go and smoke that stuff in yer bedroom,
it meks the place stink.

I'll dee what I want in me room, divvent ye start acting
the polis wi me.

Mam rubs her temples, reaches for her tabs
Kylie slams the door: I'm sick of all of ye, I'm gannin forra walk
and Dad says: I'm just poppin out an all, er, see yer later pet.

December

All the houses have their decs up, right ?
windows wi flashy dots
doors wi fairy lights all round
in each living room
yer can see a tree, wi tinsel
green and gold baubles
an I think everyone feels bright
'cept me.

An I stop at the top of Byker Hill
this one house, right, wins prizes
raises cash for good causes
it's amazin, Santy's swayin
in his sleigh in the air
there's a group of carol singers
under a lamp on the grass
three wise men and angels
in the porch, all shiny
and in the middle of the lawn
a stable wi lambs
a donkey, and a glowin mary
holding a tiny doll.
An I know it's only cheesy plastic
that it's all 60 watt bulbs
an that, but in a funny way
it seems to say
even babies born wi no walls around them
in the middle of winter wi no proper dad
are ok.

The Jayasinha's son's first Christmas

I have never seen Christmas before.
It changes this place:
These people
let cars burn on their grass
dogs foul their paths
paper grow in their gardens
but now
they have silver lights
round their windows
angels and red berries
on their doors.
People who
did not know our name
never said hello
now
they have a smile on their face
and a greeting on their lips.
I have never had a Christmas present before
now I have one
on my doorstep
a pigeon with no head
a note saying:
HAPPY XMAS
IT'S YOU NEXT
GRASS

At the doctors

There's a crowded christmas waiting room
tinsel chains criss cross the entrance hall
wooden chairs line the walls
an electronic notice board continuously displays
patients' names punctuated with a pair of bells
a sprig of holly and the words:
Festive Greetings to all our Patients.
Betty and Doris see the nurse for their flu jabs
young mams with barking babies
full of coughs and colds
single men in donkey jackets, overalls, flat caps
fitting in appointments
before the Health Centre closes.

Two chairs face each other
across the table of Health News and Hello's,
Mrs Jayasinha and Mam.
Mam flicks through last year's magazines
Mrs Jayasinha pulls her scarf tighter
so her face can barely be seen
aware, but not staring.
They are called together
to different rooms.
Inside, doctors
listen to their stories
and prescribe medication
that will numb the stress
for these women, help them to cope
to carry on, but cannot
touch the cause of their distress
or give them much hope
for a different life.

Scotty's Blue Diz-zee Xmas

Get on down in the house 2 nite,
we're tekkin you hi
feel the vibration comin on strong
we're ready 2 fly

Jump 2 the beat now, Jump 2 the beat
now everybody Rock
Minna minna mental bounce around
we take U 2 the top

get out your seat, 'n feel the heat,
comin at yer people, on your feet
move like this, get off yer face,
c'mon people we're on yer case

Kick kick, kick the mike 2 bitz
we're gonna spin
your hardcore hitz
comin on strong
comin on comin on
minna minna movin,
move along

Rock, rock with the after shock
Here's Big up massive for the Byker crew
we're comin at you
for a Diz-zee Blue christmas !

Feel the vibe now, stay alive
izzee wizz ee, letz get bizzee
get blue diz-zee
now

Somewhere

a lad lies
his eyes
go out
like lights
in a house
at night,
his mouth
a front door
that won't close,
his voice
a whisper
of wind
no-one hears
as he calls
Ma.

The phone call

It's 6 am and Kylie's asleep
I'll be there for you
drifts into her dreams
her mobile is ringing
she gropes under clothes.
Aye ?
Eyes shut

Kylie ?
Help me.

Scot, is that you ?
Eyes wide open.
A pink teddy dressing gown
tiptoes to the balcony
hair flowing once again
drops down the keys
she shushes:
don't wake me Mam.

Scotty is wasted,
his eyes are black holes
hands shaking, restless,
he can't sit still,
then his cap drops forwards, his legs collapse
in a heap on her floor
careless he lies, like a pile of clothes
on makeup, underwear, hairbrush

Shit, oh shit
Scotty starts to cry

Coming down to earth

I was doing a set
massive loud
the club the crowd
yer couldn't move man, Kylie
it we
he took five we
all did but Lee
it was dark in the
corner
I didn't realise
we didn't none of us
where he was

The Bastards said Leave him.
two hours, two fuckin hours
Lee was blue, swear down, I couldn't wake him
I tried and tried
they wouldn't call a bastard ambulance
said he'll sleep it off

Me and Shabber we dragged
dragged dragged
him to the door he didn't move
wouldn't open his eyes
I shouted bastards

scared shittin meself - he was so heavy
they wouldn't lift a fuckin finger
he was foamin his mouth
oh shit
two hours, man ! we might
mebbes if...
The bizzies were cruisin

we left him on the pavement

I need a bong man,
Kylie I feel like death.

Christmas morning visit

They sit in a row
on the settee
Mam and Dad
Sean and his tag,
Scotty holding a mug of tea
Kylie perched on the arm.
Opposite is a young CID
shaven, suited, clean
his eyes serious
as he coughs and speaks:
I'm DC Green
Do you know why I'm here ?
Sean, Mam and Dad sit dumb
Scotty says quietly, Have yer come
about what happened at the club ?
That's right - the incident at the Blue Dizzee
on the night of December 23rd.
The young man in the incident, Lee
is dead.

Dad takes off his glasses, rubs them on his shirt
Mam overflows, Oh god, so young.
Scotty is pale, he whispers, shit.
Kylie looks at him, remembers what he said.
Sean breathes in, thinks about Lee -
then he's aggressive, he knows his rights
I was home, I was fuckin here last night.
Says DC Green, We know,
and holds up something silver, blue
Is this your mobile phone ?
We found it on the lad in question
among other, he coughs, possessions.
I'm afraid we'll need you both down the station
to answer questions. Given

the serious nature of this investigation
I have to caution you: You do not have to -
But Sean's heard it once too often
he's up on his feet and Dad's up too,
holding his arm
speaking words to keep him calm,
but Mam is furious, won't let this lie.
What's this te de with our Sean ?
Yer always pickin on the lad
he's been in all the time, he's tellt yer
and I'm tellin yer he's not a murderer !
Our Sean's not that bad
but he's got nee chance of doin right
with you callin him day and night
why don't you leave him alone ?
I'm fuckin sick of you lot
comin round all the time !
Mam don't, Kylie gasps
but Mam's pummelling DC Green
on the chest, shouting,
he holds her fists
Calm down Missus
this won't help.
We need to know what happened to Lee.
Call the Duty Solicitor.
I'm afraid they're coming with me.

The blow

Flickering light from the wide screen
picks out Scot's Dad, his grim face is green
he's in his underpants, watching the match
now and then he looks at his watch,
a saucer of tab ends, a half-eaten takeaway
empty cans crowd his feet, he kicks them away.

His team are losing, he's feeling sore
when Scot and his Mam creep in the front door.
Scotty's Mam's tired, like a drowning woman,
his Dad grips a can, tips the last of it down,
C'm ere Scot.
Scot and his Mam look at each other
Scotty's white face pleads with his mother
The poor lad's shattered, we've been there all day.
but Scot's Dad pushes her out the way
like a piece of nothing he barely sees.
Scot ? What's gannin on ?
Dad, please. I wanna lie down.
Lie down is it ?
and with a quick swipe
he knocks Scot back against the wall.
Scot cracks his head, slips and falls
Dad drags him up
with the front of his jacket:
Who sold that packet ter Lee
You're gonna tell me
where you got them Ees,
and smashes his fist into Scotty's mouth
who stutters and stumbles
dribbling spittle and blood
Don't, don't... understand
but his words are stopped by his Dad's giant hand.

Scot's head is aching, he sees sunbursts and stripes
he's holding his hand up, makes muffled cries
Scotty's Mam is secretly making a call
phoning the polis, nearly fainting with fear
then she hears heavy footsteps
come down the hall.

Next door

Scot's face is a shambles,
Scot's Mam rambles:

It was a wedding present -
his Mam,
one of a set -
did she know how I might need
knives ?
Just small
but sharp,
it slipped in so easily
just like butter...
he makes a row about that
low fat stuff...

I picked it up on the spur
when he came down the hall
I didn't think... didn't mean..

The light was behind him
thin as a blade
he was, in sillhouette,
he didn't see my hand
as he walked towards me.
So much blood..
he stumbled away...
we came here...

Hinny
I've heard it all before.
Is Scot alright ? Are you alright ?
Would yez both like a cuppa ?

Mrs Jayasinha leaves the wall

It's been cold this winter.
Not like Home. Here they say too cold for real snow,
like dust on the wall and walkways, thin
like my coat. Brian says we have to go.
It's for the best, he says. Pack up your things
put them by the door. I'll load the car.
We wait for him in my kind neighbour's house
in her little kitchen. I have a cup of tea.
My husband stares into the table surface.
My neighbour is sad, she says my face is ghostly.
She gives me half a christmas cake
a scarf for my boy.
She says
I must do something -
build my confidence. After this place.
Like leaving prison.

Leftovers

The table has a sorry look
a melted candle, torn paper hats
mottos and jokes crumpled on the mat
Dad's got his nose in a book about pigeons
Nana's helping Mam tidy up in the kitchen,
Kylie is nibbling a giant toblerone,
Sean is angry about his mobile phone.

Who wants a turkey sandwich or another mince pie ?
Mam calls from the kitchen but gets no reply
no-one is talking; there's too much to say,
Nana brings in mugs of tea on a brown plastic tray.

They all sit and watch TV, The Wizard of Oz
but no-one's really listening
because
because
because

The funeral

Hard rain is stotting
grey sky lowers itself onto roofs
black cars move slow and heavy
black wet pavements splash with feet.

A crowd is gathering at the Crem
waiting to be let in
umbrellas and newspapers the only shelter.
Lee's Mam has sunglasses on
a black suited man is supporting her arm.
Sean and the lads smoke tabs
heads down, backs to the world
shaven headed, pasty white
not talking,
Kylie and the Bella Brigade are weeping
on each others shoulders
holding flowers and pictures of Lee
add them to the growing pile
at the door of the crem;
wreathed chyrsanths spell:
GOOD-BYE LEE
IN MEMORY OF A LOVING SON
Soggy Tags read
All our Love, Aunty June
We'll miss you Lee, the Byker Lasses

Kylie catches eyes with Scotty, sees his bruised face
one quick glance, then they look away,
there's nothing to say.

Mam and Dad in raincoats stand
at the edge of the crowd with Nana
sombre and silent, minds replaying
another funeral a year before.
Mam holds a hanky to her nose and sobs soundlessly
Nana's eyes trickle with pain
Dad looks up as if expecting
a sign from the heavens.

Going round to Lee's Mam after

She sways on the settee,
smoking and drinking like it's her dying act,
lips clamp round the tip of a bottle
sucking hard, snorting smoke.
Refuses tea, with a wave of her tab
not really listening
to sympathy.

Poor lad, she says,
poor … poor... Lee
Wha'ma gonna do without im ?
He was good t'me.
Thanks fer comin.

Pursing her lips, biting her cheeks
tipping her head back,

Wha'ma gonna do ?

she says to no-one,
eyes flicker side to side,
looking for something,
someone, looking strangled.

For Auld Lang Syne

Mam's on Prozac,
Dad drinks pints of tea
Kylie cuddles a coke bottle,
Nana, a single malt whisky

while in the other room
Sean is having
a cocktail

Ecstasy
Speed
Magic Mushrooms
Weed
Stella
Baileys
Cough mixture
Tabs

On a skitz

Sean's flipped, lost it, he's in a red rage
he smashes, smashes the wall of his cage.

He's dropping dinner plates one by one
over the balcony, Mam's had to run
smash smash smash smash

she's in the toilet, too scared to come out
shivery, weeping, hears Sean shout

I've got the TV
The Bizzies use it to spy on me
Kerasshh !
He blasts a hole in the front glass window
the tv explodes on the concrete below.
He grabs the breadknife, stabs the settee
the cushions, the curtains all torn to shreds
Riip, riip rip rippp
He yanks the phone line out of the wall
That'll fuck the black bastards listenin, he bawls.
Spisssh, Spisssh - he's got the foam cleaner
sprays shiny surfaces til they're misty and green
accuses the mirror above the sink
of peepholes and cameras, video links.
He hammers the wall, yells through the door
You're gettin it too, I'm gonna get yer.

Then it goes quiet;

Mam waits half an hour, unlocks the catch
she's walking slowly on broken glass
her face a cracked mirror,
reflecting the devastation in the flat.
With unsteady hands, she opens the front door
taps quietly on her neighbour's window
who peeps through her nets, then lets her in.

AWOL

Away in his head
Alone. Escaped.
On top of the world
icy snow flakes his eyes, clouds for a cap
wind for a muffler, a coat of leaves.
He ran away from the flat.
Didn't he ?
Absent, without leave.

Down in the dark
without light,
ploughed mud,
bushes in the park
hiding, did he ?

Gone awol.
He's Free.
Isn't he ?

No - Hospital.
Yes.

Now he's
staring at walls
He's been nicked
square, solid. Slow his feet
cold his hands. Bed metal white.
No paints, bare walls
bare soul
St Nicks,
nothing escapes here
he's
absent   minded

absent

gone.

What Sean sees from his hospital bed

slippers, tartan, big
they slop about after him

someone's hands
fat and floppy, they lie in his lap all day

his Dad's glasses
and a little bit of elastoplast stuck on the edge

he watches that elastoplast,
sit still, move about

it makes him want to shout
he waves his arms about

someone is crying, there's a fat woman
the ceiling, it's cream, blank

he dreams of putting something on it
he smiles

he sees the inside of his eyes pinky red
in his dream someone says

Goodnight son
but his tongue is tied and he can't answer

Kylie gets cabin fever

Mam's at the hospital
Dad's at the crees
Sean's off his heed,
what about me ?
On me tod
watching daytime tv,
who can I talk to ?
Sammi's at school.
I'm just hanging round
I feel a right fool

stuck in this flat
bored out me skull
how sad is that ?

I'm scared that it'll all go wrong.

Maybe the baby'll be
a handful like Sean ?
Or worse ?
I'm gannin spare
so

I ring Scotty's mobile and all
I get is this voice like it's miles away:
the mobile phone you have called
is switched off.

Kylie hoys a wobbler

I look like one of them
wifies from weightwatchers
who wear minging things,
nothing fits. I cannot go out.

I'll get yer a new top, says Mam

Nah. What's th' point ?

Ye'll not be like it forever, Kylie.

I will. Just look at ye !
I'd rather kill meself than end up like that.
Yer fat an' stupid. Yer kna nowt -

Kylie !

Useless and stupid. Yer let Sean de owt he likes,
but yer hate me. It's your fault
this family's a mess.
Yer never lissen ter me. Not like Nana.
Her Mam was the same.
Sent Nana away
because…

Because ?... Haway... Kylie, lookit me...

Aye. See. Yer don't know everything.
Nana wouldn't tell ye, but she
told me !

What the hell are you on about ?

Nana and Mam have a talk

Hen, yer still ma daughter
I never thought to tell ye
go upsetting things.
It wiz a lang time ago
I wiz jest a wee lassie
Kylie brought it all back

What about me Da ?

We never talked of it
too painful, but he stood by me
no word of blame or shame.

What about Nan in Aberdeen ?

Nan and him didn't see eye to eye.
Her religion would stick in his craw
she thought his left wing views bore the mark of the devil.
He'd sing Burns songs to rile her.
She wanted to pretend it never happened,
I never could reconcile her to it.

Kylie says I'm like your Mam

No hen,
it was different then.
Your Nan wiz strict
rigid aboot b'liefs
I had te deal with it
on ma oan, far from home,
you're there for Kylie.
She needs ye,
whatever she says now.

I wonder where he is now ? My brother, I mean.

Aye.

The Jayasinha's third new home

They stand in a dark hall
with cardboard boxes
that contain
their short English life:
one pair of curtains
three plates, knives and forks
assorted books
a battered suitcase of clothes.
Mrs Jayasinha holds
a Morrison's plastic bag
with spices from the far east
and a cooking pot,
their travelling kitchen.
Mr Jayasinha embraces his wife
grasps his son's arms
smiles at him
then starts to unpack.

Kylie has an unexpected visit

Hiya Shabber, hev yer come to see our Sean ?

Na, I've come ter paint yer window,

Oh,

I'm on a cooncil scheme
I do one day release at college too,

Oh aye ? D'yer like it ?

Na, I'm thinking of jackin it in.
Gettin up in the cad mornins
man, it's a killer
an the pay's shite.

Oh, right,
well, it's in here.

I cannot de nowt til me supervisor gets here.

Oh

How's Sean, anyways ?

Ok... Gettin better.
Yer can visit if yer want.

Aye ?

D'yer want a cuppa, while yer wait, like ?

Aye, ta.

New Year's resolution

Kylie has a number to ring.
The Welfare wifey
says it's to help girls like her.
Kylie says nowt
but thinks the Welfare Wifey knows nowt
about girls like her.

A friendly voice tells her
to come to the office in the city centre
the voice says she must fill in forms;
Kylie bites her lip.
The voice is saying words like
Alternative Education,
Ante-Natal check-ups
financial situation,
long, hard, grown-up words.

Kylie doesn't want to go
Dad says he'll come with her
if she wants.

On the metro
she sees Scotty, who reddens
and looks away.
As she gets off, she whispers:
I'm having it in May.

Scotty looks up and beams.

Assessment

Mam and Dad are on the edge
of their seats
the man in a white coat
leans over his,
he's looking at notes
he's looking grim,
he shuffles his papers
says Thanks for coming in.
Mam asks How's Sean ?
Is he getting better ?
The psychiatrist pauses
taps his fingertips together
I need to assess
why Sean's so aggressive.
Tell me about him.

The Young Mums 2B Group

Kylie sits on a big brown sofa
trying to get comfortable;
her baby is wriggling, she feels a foot
kick out, she gasps quietly
she will bear this in silence.

She looks around,
three other girls
with glum faces
mugs of coffee
and stomachs like drums,
stare at one another
noncommittal, not sure why they've come.

A big woman in a T shirt with Rita on the front
and Great North Run, is busy on the phone,
on the wall are posters:
zero tolerance for domestic violence,
smoking harms your baby
drug information and pictures of contraceptives.
One girl gets up: I'm not stayin here,
youse can all Fuck Off.
All eyes swivel to Rita
she smiles and puts down the phone
Come on Tracey, finish your coffee,
give it a chance. Let's start
with names.

Names

What yer gonna call it ? Dawn looks up at her.
Kylie's in her room, lying on her bed
Sammi and Dawn rest their heads against it
drinking tea and eating Wagon Wheels.
Gorrany tabs ? Kylie holds out her hand
I thought you were stoppin ? says Sammi
Aye, well ... I cut doon... but I'm gaggin
Gan on says Dawn and lights her one.
They watch blue smoke curl through the shadows,

Can't think of any names.
Kylie man, there's hods...
Posh and Becks called theirs after where they did it, giggles
Sammi
I'd have ter call it Bedroom, then.
Or Flat 27
Meet my son, Byker Wall.
What if it's a girl ?
Shields Road, of course.
they laugh.
I can't think of any, cos I can't imagine havin it
a real bairn.
They sit, trying to imagine.

Kylie talks with Mam

Mam's sitting with a tab, reading the Chronicle
her feet up on the pouffe
Yer hev to she says
Why ?
Mam sighs, Because... without looking up,
Because WHAT ?
Mam drops her paper on her lap,
Because, Kylie
she points at her with two fingers and the tab
ohforgodsake,
yer mek me so tired.
An I can't be arsed with you neither.
Because... you're the only friend he's got.
He's lonely in there, no-one ter visit him
'cept me an yer Dad.
Nana can go.
She does, but not one of his pals.
I'm worried.   He's so low.
An he lost two of his best mates
in the last few months: Scot then .. Lee.
What's that got ter de with me ? shouts Kylie
Mam just looks at her
with a face
like thunder.

Visiting Time

I bought yer some tabs

Ta

....Feelin ok ?

Aye

I've been thinkin about Granda.

Aye.

What he used ter say.
What closes when it opens
and what's only open when it's closed ?
He loved ter tease us wi' riddles.

Aye.

Remember he took us to see
the giant floating crane ?

Asian Hercules.   Aye.

Aye. Yer acted cool, but I knew
yer wer excited.
Us all together,
seein it carry the new bridge up the Tyne.

Biggest in the world.
Only see that once in a lifetime, Granda said.

It was sunny, November,
the water was dead flat.
Once he carried me like that.
Now, when I walk across the new Eye bridge
I always remember Granda.

I used ter think he was a giant.

Mrs Jayasinha invites Nana round

Nana's in a quiet part of town
trying to track down the right address.
She pushes a bell that doesn't ring
she knocks gently then firmer
Mrs Jayasinha opens the door
smiles and pulls Nana in,
Welcome, welcome !
Nana looks at her, draped in midnight blue
How are ye hen ?
They share cups of tea
on the shabby settee
Nana asks about the family
but thinks
Mrs J is looking thin;
I've made yer some wee fairy cakes
Nana holds out a biscuit tin
Mrs Jayasinha smiles Lovely cake, thank you
but doesn't eat.
She says she knows no-one in the street
but doesn't mind,
her son likes his new school
his teacher is the kind that makes them
work hard.
This is good.   He will pass exams.
Study. Get a better job.
He will be happy.
Suddenly Mrs Jayasinha starts to sob
Nana puts out her hands
takes two brown thin ones
and holds them tight
wishing she could offer so much more
than cake.

Scotty visits Sean

His ears are blasting with Blue Dizzee sound
as he makes his way through the hospital grounds,

daffodils hip-hop in the wind,
a buzz entry voice lets him in.

His trainers squeak on the well-polished tiles
as he stops a young man with an armful of files:

I'm looking for Sean. Yeah, try room number three
if he's not in there, he'll be somewhere around.

Scot's not prepared for the changes in Sean
he's plump, and he's slow, he's calmed right down.

Alreet mate ? as they sit drinking tea
Yeah smiles Sean, pleased to see him.

I bought yer this and hands Sean a packet
inside is Sean's mobile, an official police docket.

They're not pressing charges, we're all in the clear,
ye've nothing to face when ye get out of here.

But what did they say about what happened ter Lee ?
the bouncers, the owners at the Blue Diz-zee ?

Polis got nee witnesses, got nee proof
nothing to show Lee died under their roof.

Me, Dez and Shabber wouldn't say owt.
Got more sense than to open me mouth.

But - begins Sean. Just leave it at that.
I'm gannin, says Scot, Da's expecting me back.

All the best, mate, I'll see yer soon.
When yer out, I'll get tickets for the Toon, eh ?

Kylie meets the Bella Brigade

I'm gettin fat like me Ma
Dawn and Sammi, Debbie and Jo
chorus No !
Yer gonna have a bairn, man, Kylie.
It's normal

Kylie grabs a handful of flesh
Lookit me arse !

Dawn and Debbie laugh
but Kylie is serious

What if I stay like this after ?
What sort of Mam will I be ?
What if I end up on happy pills ?

They all sit silent, smoke drifting round
the empty pavilion in the park,
slowly the afternoon sun scrapes the trees
it gets dark.

What if I'm like Scotty's Mam ?
Dawn says Skinny as a pencil
Flat as paper, Sammi agrees

Kylie says And crumples easily an all.
Eeh god, what if Scotty's like his Dad ?
Yer kna, drinking, violent
ter me and the bairn ?

Nah, man Kylie, Jo says Scotty's ok

Yer divvent kna - havin a bairn
might change him, change me ?

Sammi says Yer might be like yer Nana
Dawn tuts and shakes her head
but Kylie thinks
maybe that wouldn't be so bad.

A meeting in JJ's

The cafe in Byker opposite Kwiksave
it's quiet on a Tuesday morning
whispers Scotty on his mobile
It'll be safe.

Kylie waits in a corner, and watches;
the sickly yellow walls are grubby
the green/black carpet stained
a heater is held to the wall
with stretchy hooks, the melamine table
is fixed to the floor.
The chairs are second-hand office stock
metal but comfier than they look
the table hides her growing bump.

On the wall beside her is a print
called April Love - a girl in blue
stands in a leafy corner
she has ringlets and a secret smile.
Kylie stirs her mug of tea
stares at a pale blue plastic high chair
stacked in a corner.

Two men read papers with their breakfast stotties
three women chat, with their first tab of the day
walnut faced, thin as wire, yet their coughs
would rip a man apart, she thinks.
A schoolboy loiters, shirt untucked
tie loosely knotted, trying to show he's got a tab;
she wishes she were somewhere else,
her spirits sink, then the door opens
and in slinks Scotty.

He smiles sheepishly, she grins back
they start to talk.

Kylie, still dreaming

I'm lying on this big table
in a dark room
a bright light shines on me
there's blood
all ower me giant belly
an I'm havin it
this, this thing
with two black holes
fer eyes and a blue face
and out its mouth
like a tongue
snakin round and round its neck
stranglin it
there's this wet gurglin sound
I know it's drownin
but I can't reach it
a big Polis comes
with black gloved hands
says I'm tekkin that
an I cannot stop him
I'm fixed ter the table
I cannot shout
nowt,
no sound comes out me mouth
then I wake up
sweatin.
An I'm scared.

Nana has an idea for Sean

Kill two birds with one stone, eh ?
Maybe that's no the right way
to put it, but I've spoken to them all
Community Police, Brian,
the Youth team, the YMCA.
It's about building trust and painting walls,
new links between us, and them.
Fer you, it's proof
that you can mend yer ways
I know ye can, yer no a bad lad
really.

A chilly Saturday, spitting rain
finds Sean in overalls, cans of paint
in both hands, waiting
by the padlocked Centre door.
Brian says Y'alreet mate ?
wielding a big bunch of keys
and gives a grin; across the road
a small group hesitate
Brian waves them in
Mr Jayasinha's son among them,
all come to decorate the precious space
spared for the Refugees.
Sean hopes no-one saw him going in.

Dad looks out the window of his cree

It's all about desire. Getting the birds to return.
They'll hurry if they know there's a pretty dove
waiting on their perch.

Across the river, I can see the new art gallery
red brick, Baltic in big letters,
I remember when it was a flour mill.
Everything's changed, it's confusing,
the look of things can fool you
like us - married
but it doesn't feel like we are.

There's the millennium bridge, smart folk
walking up and down, looking for something
art I suppose, a new feeling.
We're in different worlds, different universe
like an invisible wall between us:
I don't belong there, and they
never see me.
It feels like that with her, too.
Maybe she can't see a new use
for me ?

How is it I can get pigeons to come back
but not my wife ?

Sean plays 5 a side with Brian

Hey, ye,
baldy-heeded bastard
gorra smoke ?
gorrany tack ?

Are ye gannin te play or what
pass,
pass man, howay !
nash on
belter
hey, ye'v knacked us man

bollicks - pass,
gan on
shoot, shoot,
Yess
Goal !

Ha we got footy next week ?
I divvent give a shit.
Givis five ye baldy git.

The last straw

Sean's feeling good, he shoulders his bag,
stops in the arch, lights up his tab,
graffiti for Brian, he's planning a big one
the whole of a wall is going to be done.

Then a hand on his shoulder stops him in his tracks
two bizzies take his bag, Sean barks Give it back !
Well, well, it's ACEE. They hear paint cans clink,
they rattle the rucksack, Where d'you think

you're going with this ? What're yer planning to do ?
A nice little hoard. Black, red and blue.
To be on the safe side, I think we'll take these.
Sean's getting angry, he's not going to say Please.

I'm gannin doon the centre, to paint a wall
Brian asked me ter de it, yer can ask him an' all.
No time. We've appointments. Call in next week
We'll keep them safe, at Clifford Street. Alreet ?

Sean's feeling helpless, he's near to despair
the bizzies just grin, he radges   It's not fair !
then the old anger rises up in a rush
he loses his head, he gives a big push
at the bastard who's holding his precious paint
then Sean swings the punch that seals his fate.

What it's like

I'm tellin yer, right ?
I'm walkin in the park
thinkin about our Sean
slow like, because this baby
weighs a ton,
and I'm feelin like it's never gonna come.
In the distance
is this young lass with a German Shepherd
suddenly it's an arrow racin for me
an I'm like, shit, what am a gonna de ?
But it shoots past me
there's this other owd wifey
with a massive rottweiler
an the two dogs are barkin
hungry like they wanna eat each other
all snarlin teeth an that
an the owd wifey drags her lead
but the rottweiler's much stronger
an the lass is runnin shoutin Rocky, Rockee !
the dogs are fightin, turnin round an round
a ball of fur an slaverin tongues.

An I think they probly got them for protection, right ?
But they got no control,
the lass is screechin Rockee desprit, her voice gettin higher
the owd wifey's barkin King Down Down boy
they're helpless
an the dogs just gan on an on barkin and fightin

An I walk away. Yeah
That's what it's like.

Scotty's back at the Blue Diz-zee

It's MC Master !
Coming on strong,
c'mon people
witha bucket ana bong

c'mon people
givus a shout
gettin Blue Dizzee's
what it's all about

fuck the bizzies
hear the sound
spinning vynal
goin round

minna minna movin
to the beat
bidda bidda bad boys
in the street

MC Master
Underground
Yessa Yessa
nash on down

In the dark

Kylie remembers, long ago
under the covers
of a different bed
feeling scared
in winter's metallic cold
smelling train brakes;
ship hooters moaned
orange street light
crept weirdly
through curtains,
she shut her eyes
explored teddy
with blind fingertips.

Now she feels
her swollen belly
hard and weird
hears herself moan
this train is coming
her eyes roll back
hair a damp curtain
she tastes metal fear
grips her Mam's fingers
as they creep
towards the light
at the end
of this blind red
tunnel.

Out of the tunnel

A brisk Irish midwife has a feel, a quick laugh
snaps off her gloves: Sure, you've a while yet,
how about a nice bath ?
Mam, I'm sc...
Shh, c'mon.
They find a small bathroom, glowing and pink
with a giant old bath, which fills fast to the brink.
Kylie takes off T shirt, loosens trackie bottoms and trainers
Mam folds them like she used to when Kylie was six
and Kylie sinks into warm water. They wait, a clock ticks.

Eyes closed, almost dozing,
two hours pass in a daze
then Kylie grips the bath sides
her eyes glaze:
I want to go home
There there, says Mam
she's pouring warm water
over this restless whale
who's breathing and cursing
and blowing a gale,
Another one over, it'll soon be here
I don't want to have it
You're doin great, cheer up
Mam looks at this girl
in the grip of a contraction
remembers sixteen years ago,
how it's passed in a fraction.
You were tiny, five pounds
slipped out so easy
as she pours and pours water
like waves on a shore.

But suddenly Kylie's queasy
Mam, Mam ! I need a shit
her eyes roll back, she grits her teeth.
Maybe it's comin ? Mam is alarmed
Not in the bath ! she takes Kylie's arm
helps her out, wraps her up
in a huge fluffy towel: I'll get the midwife
Don't leave me ! Kylie howls
Kylie waddles slowly to the ante-natal room
wearing a nightie that won't close at the back
the midwife waits for a contraction to slacken
she has a good feel, a look, a listen:
Everything's fine, the baby's heartbeat is strong
into the delivery suite, it'll be along shortly,
I want drugs, says Kylie, I want it out of there !
Too late, me darlin, you can have gas and air.

Kylie sucks in the mask
like a woman possessed
won't let it go
she's getting distressed
Fucking Baby ! she shouts
Mam says Shush
Nearly there, says the midwife
one more push

Push Push says Mam
There ! see its head ?
but Kylie just moans
It's takin too long
the midwife gets a mirror
holds it angled, says See
that wee tangled mass of curls ?

Is that comin out of me ?

Pant… push.. pant as the baby arrives
Well done pet, Mam smiles then cries.

Kylie cries too, with exhaustion then hoys up
as the midwife holds the bundle in her arms:
It's a boy.

Getting a life

she holds him
like a net of oranges
his head lolls
she fears it will drop off
if she doesn't keep it in her hands.
It fits
but has she arms enough
for all the loose limbs of him
that dangle or disappear
into the clothes
he nests inside ?
She strokes long feet
blood orange velour
a first try at shape, not quite sorted
and the pink grapefruit of his head
mouth and eyes closed slits
that snap open to bawl.
Kylie is appalled
how he grips with his suck
scared by how strong
this love feels.

Text

Scotty
itza boy
26.5.04
drk hr
bth ok
cu
K

What Kylie sees from her hospital bed

Dad's holdin it
like it's a prize he's just won
his face's a giant smiley
says Hello, Pigeon an kisses
his soft feathery hair.
Mam's watching Dad
in a new way,
but all she says is Haway,
let the grandma have a turn
Dad looks at Mam
gives her the bundle
and out the window
the sun is brilliant on the green leaves
on the trees in the park.

In a park

in another part of town
the Jayasinha family walk
watching rabbits, a cockerel, hens
animals in pens.
Father and son talk, serious.
A little way behind
Mrs Jayasinha follows
she's wearing a dress
of gold and yellow
under an old brown coat
pulled close round,
a faraway look
on her hollow face.

Dad and Mam talk

Remember I took yer te the coast ?
Yer were fond of Cullercoats Bay
I thought it'd soften yer to the idea -
bit romance, the beach
little ripplin waves, big harvest moon
round as the ring I kept fingerin
in me pocket.
I was that nervous
I thought ye'd say no.
We'd had a fish supper at Marshall's
and walked along from the Trafalgar.
Could I say it ?
I was bletherin about anything, nowt.

An I said Sshh

So we sat on the beach and watched the sea
tipped in silver moonlight.
Then yer slipped yer hand in mine
I took that as a good sign
an I plucked up courage
said Well ? What about you and me ?
I got the ring out
and dropped it in the sand
yer bugger an hell !

An I laughed

A man's a man for a' that

Ye de yer best
Ye dinna ken what Fate has in store fer ye.
Is the wurld a better place ?
Oor dreams, have they come true ?

We used to sing to th' weans
when we sat under sleepless stars
waiting for their fathers to return
from sea, from under thi earth,
from th' high spans or th' bellies of ships.
All those thoosands of men
their boots crackin on the pavin stones
where are they noo ?

Aye, I've seen changes.
Here's tall walls and cascades of ivy,
once it was back-to-back
and a waterfall of voices down these banks.

When I was a wee lass
my Pa took me te the library
each week he said I had to get three books:
one novel, one history and one biography.
He said Hen - Libraries are there fer all
and readin is free.
That's the best education I can giv ye.
An I see them closin the libraries noo
it fair meks me despair.

Still, I get up every mornin
while ye can struggle
there's always a wee bit of hope.

And baby makes...

Scotty and Kylie meet in the Dene
sit on a bench where they can't be seen,
Scott has the baby on his knee
he says cooee
Kylie says How's yer Dad ?
she chews her gum, a bubble smacks
I divvent give a toss about that
I'm gettin me flat and
he can't say nowt about it.
This is my bairn. I'm old enough.
He waves a finger
for the baby to hold
Me ma said to give yer this.
Kylie unfolds something cream and lacy
It was me christening shawl
me ma said the bairn should have it.
Aye ? It's special like
She says she'll babysit
if yer want her to.
Aye. That's canny,
and they watch the Ouseburn
sharing a can of coke,
a smoke
and the baby
in turns.

A postcard never sent from Gilsland Maternity Hospital, 1943

Dearest Ma, this is the view from my window
brown fields, green hills, no houses or shops
a few trees, all bent like tired women
and miles of empty landscape
dotted with sheep and lambs.
I hear them bleating.
The gardens are covered with yellow crocus
but the wind sharpens the weather.
The extra rations of milk and orange juice are good
but some of the wee things are in wicker clothes baskets
for lack of cradles. Matron doesn't smile
like she does with the married ones
just hands me a mop and bucket,
says And I mean clean, mind.

You said not to write, but that's alright
because I haven't got a pen or a postcard
and my room doesn't have a window.
I just wish I could have shown you
my little lamb, then I know
you would have wanted me to keep him.